JONATHAN EDWARDS
LOVER OF GOD

THE ESSENTIAL
EDWARDS
COLLECTION

OWEN STRACHAN *and* DOUGLAS SWEENEY

MOODY PUBLISHERS
CHICAGO

Editor: Christopher Reese
Interior Design: Ragont Design
Cover Design: Gearbox

Library of Congress Cataloging-in-Publication Data

Strachan, Owen.
    Jonathan Edwards, lover of God / Owen Strachan and Douglas Sweeney.
    p. cm. — (The essential Edwards collection)
    Includes bibliographical references.
    ISBN 978-0-8024-2457-0
    1. Edwards, Jonathan, 1703-1758. 2. Congregational churches--United States—Clergy—Biography. I. Sweeney, Douglas A. II. Title.
BX7260.E3S77 2009
285.8092—dc22
[B]

                                                            2009040808

We hope you enjoy this book from Moody Publishers. Our goal is to provide high-quality, thought-provoking books and products that connect truth to your real needs and challenges. For more information on other books and products written and produced from a biblical perspective, go to www.moodypublishers.com or write to:

Moody Publishers
820 N. LaSalle Boulevard
Chicago, IL 60610

1 3 5 7 9 10 8 6 4 2

Printed in the United States of America

These primers on Jonathan Edwards's life and thought—his passion for God—provide an excellent glimpse into a life lived unto God. And they help the rest of us slake our thirst for the majesty of our Savior. We owe a great debt to Owen Strachan and Douglas Sweeney for making Edwards and his vision of God so accessible to the rest of us thirsty pilgrims.

> —**Thabiti Anyabwile**, Pastor of First Baptist Church of Grand Cayman, Cayman Islands

Everyone says Jonathan Edwards is important. Quite frankly, however, his writing style is pretty dense by contemporary standards, so few pastors and other Christian leaders have invested much time reading him. This new series tackles the problem. Here is the kernel of much of Edwards's thought in eminently accessible form.

> —**D. A. Carson**, Research Professor of New Testament, Trinity Evangelical Divinity School

In *The Essential Edwards Collection*, Owen Strachan and Doug Sweeney point with knowledge and excitement to clear and searching sections that illuminate God's truth and search our hearts. In this collection, Edwards is introduced to a new generation of readers. His concerns are made our concerns. This is a worthy effort and I pray that God will bless it.

> —**Mark Dever**, Senior Pastor, Capitol Hill Baptist Church, Washington, DC

I am deeply impressed with the vision that has brought together this splendid library of volumes to introduce Jonathan Edwards to a new generation. Owen Strachan and Douglas Sweeney have provided an incredible service by making the often challenging writings of America's greatest theologian accessible for seasoned theologians, pastors, and students alike with their five-volume *Essential Edwards Collection*. This series is properly titled the "essential collection."

> —**David S. Dockery**, President, Union University

This series is a fantastic introduction to the heart, mind, and ministry of the greatest theologian America has ever produced.

—**Mark Driscoll**, Pastor of Mars Hill Church, President of the Acts 29 Church Planting Network

Jonathan Edwards was a preacher of the Word, a pastor of souls, a philosopher of first rank, and the greatest theologian America has ever produced. In this wonderful new anthology of Edwards's writings, the great Puritan saint lives again. I can think of no better tonic for our transcendence-starved age than the writings of Edwards. But beware: reading this stuff can change your life forever!

—**Timothy George**, Founding Dean of Beeson Divinity School of Samford University

Let Strachan and Sweeney serve as your guides through the voluminous writings of America's greatest theologian. They have been shaped by his godly counsel and moved by his passion for Christ. By God's grace, Edwards can do the same for you. Start your journey with *The Essential Edwards Collection*.

—**Collin Hansen**, Author of *Young, Restless, Reformed*

Owen Strachan and Douglas Sweeney have done us all a great service by remixing and reloading the teaching of Jonathan Edwards for a new generation. They do more than introduce us to his writing: they show us how his biblical teaching relates to a modern world and leave us hungry for more. I am very impressed and very grateful for *The Essential Edwards Collection*.

—**Joshua Harris**, Senior Pastor of Covenant Life Church

From a course he taught at Yale and in personal friendship, Doug Sweeney has taught me much about Edwards. Possessing a command of the academic field, he and Owen Strachan nevertheless write this collection with pastoral concern, showing the relevance of Edwards for our Christian faith and practice today. It's a rare combination of gifts and insights that Sweeney and Strachan bring to this task.

> —**Michael Horton**, J. Gresham Machen Professor of Systematic Theology and Apologetics, Westminster Theological Seminary California

When it comes to Jonathan Edwards's writing, where does an average reader (like me!) begin? Right here, with *The Essential Edwards Collection*. Strachan and Sweeney provide a doorway into the life and teaching of one of the church's wisest theologians. The authors have also included notes of personal application to help us apply the life and teaching of Edwards to our own lives. I've read no better introduction to Jonathan Edwards.

> —**C. J. Mahaney**, President of Sovereign Grace Ministries

Why hasn't this been done before? *The Essential Edwards Collection* is now essential reading for the serious-minded Christian. Doug Sweeney and Owen Strachan have written five excellent and accessible introductions to America's towering theological genius—Jonathan Edwards. They combine serious scholarship with the ability to make Edwards and his theology come alive for a new generation. *The Essential Edwards Collection* is a great achievement and a tremendous resource. I can't think of a better way to gain a foundational knowledge of Edwards and his lasting significance.

> —**R. Albert Mohler Jr.**, President of The Southern Baptist Theological Seminary

A great resource! Edwards continues to speak, and this series of books is an excellent means to hear Jonathan Edwards again live and clear. Pure gold; be wise and invest in it!

> —**Dr. Josh Moody**, Senior Pastor, College Church in Wheaton.

You hold in your hands a unique resource: a window into the life and thought of Jonathan Edwards, a man whose life was captured by God for the gospel of Jesus Christ. In these pages you'll not only learn about Edwards, but you'll be able to hear him speak in his own words. This winsome and accessible introduction is now the first thing I'd recommend for those who want to know more about America's greatest pastor-theologian.

      —**Justin Taylor**, Managing Editor, ESV Study Bible

Jonathan Edwards is surely one of the most influential theologians of the eighteenth century. Now, at last, we have a wide-ranging and representative sample of his work published in an attractive, accessible and, most important of all, readable form. The authors are to be commended for the work they have put into this set and I hope it will become an important feature of the library of many pastors and students of the Christian faith.

      —**Carl R. Trueman**, Academic Dean, Westminster Theological Seminary

The Essential Edwards Collection

Jonathan Edwards: Lover of God

Jonathan Edwards on Beauty

Jonathan Edwards on Heaven and Hell

Jonathan Edwards on the Good Life

Jonathan Edwards on True Christianity

CONTENTS

ABBREVIATIONS OF
WORKS CITED

The following shortened forms of books by or about Jonathan Edwards are used in the text to indicate the source of quotations.

Kimnach, Wilson H., Kenneth P. Minkema, and Douglas A. Sweeney, eds. *The Sermons of Jonathan Edwards: A Reader*. New Haven: Yale Univ. Press, 1999.
Cited as "Kimnach" in the text.

Marsden, George. *Jonathan Edwards: A Life*. New Haven: Yale Univ. Press, 2003.
Cited as "Marsden" in the text.

Books in the Yale University Press
Works of Jonathan Edwards series

In the text, the volumes are listed in the following format: (*Works* 1, 200). The "1" refers to the series volume; the "200" refers to the page number in the given volume.

Edwards, Jonathan. *Freedom of the Will*, ed. Paul Ramsey, *The Works of Jonathan Edwards*, vol. 1. New Haven: Yale, 1957.

_____. *Religious Affections*, ed. John Smith, *The Works of Jonathan Edwards*, vol. 2. New Haven: Yale, 1959.

_____. *Original Sin*, ed. Clyde A. Holbrook, *The Works of Jonathan Edwards*, vol. 3. New Haven: Yale, 1970.

_____. *The Great Awakening*, ed. C. C. Goen, *The Works of Jonathan Edwards*, vol. 4. New Haven: Yale, 1972.

_____. *Ethical Writings*, ed. Paul Ramsay, *The Works of Jonathan Edwards*, vol. 8. New Haven: Yale, 1989.

_____. *Sermons and Discourses, 1723–1729*, ed. Kenneth E. Minkema, *The Works of Jonathan Edwards*, vol. 14. New Haven: Yale, 1997.

_____. *Notes on Scripture*, ed. Stephen Stein, *The Works of Jonathan Edwards*, vol. 15. New Haven: Yale, 1998.

_____. *Letters and Personal Writings*, ed. George S. Claghorn, *The Works of Jonathan Edwards*, vol. 16. New Haven: Yale, 1998.

_____. *Sermons and Discourses, 1730–1733*, ed. Mark Valeri, *The Works of Jonathan Edwards*, vol. 17. New Haven: Yale, 1999.

_____. *The "Miscellanies," 501–832*, ed. Ava Chamberlain, *The Works of Jonathan Edwards*, vol. 18. New Haven: Yale, 2000.

_____. *Sermons and Discourses, 1734–1738*, ed. M. X. Lesser, *The Works of Jonathan Edwards*, vol. 19. New Haven: Yale, 2001.

_____. *Sermons and Discourses, 1739–1742*, ed. Harry S. Stout and Nathan O. Hatch with Kyle P. Farley, *The Works of Jonathan Edwards*, vol. 22. New Haven: Yale, 2003.

Jonathan Edwards, a God-Entranced Man

*W*hen I was in seminary, a wise professor told me that besides the Bible I should choose one great theologian and apply myself throughout life to understanding and mastering his thought. This way I would sink at least one shaft deep into reality, rather than always dabbling on the surface of things. I might come to know at least one system with which to bring other ideas into fruitful dialogue. It was good advice.

The theologian I have devoted myself to is Jonathan Edwards. All I knew of Edwards when I went to seminary was that he preached a sermon called "Sinners in the Hands of an Angry God," in which he said something about hanging over hell by a slender thread. My first real encounter with Edwards was when I read his "Essay on the Trinity" and wrote a paper on it for church history.

It had a lasting effect on me. It gave me a conceptual framework with which to grasp, in part, the meaning of saying God is three in one. In brief, there is God the Father, the fountain of being, who from all eternity has had a perfectly clear and distinct image and idea of himself; and this image is the eternally begotten Son. Between this Son and Father there flows a stream of infinitely vigorous love and perfectly holy communion; and this is God the Spirit. God's Image of God and God's Love of God are so full of God that they are fully divine Persons, and not less.

After graduation from college, and before my wife and I took off for graduate work in Germany, we spent some restful days on a small farm in Barnesville, Georgia. Here I had another encounter with Edwards. Sitting on one of those old-fashioned two-seater swings in the backyard under a big hickory tree, with pen in hand, I read *The Nature of True Virtue*. I have a long entry in my journal from July 14, 1971, in which I try to understand, with Edwards's help, why a Christian is obligated to forgive wrongs when there seems to be a moral law in our hearts that cries out against evil in the world.

Later, when I was in my doctoral program in Germany, I encountered Edwards's *Dissertation Concerning the End for Which God Created the World*. I read it in a pantry in our little apartment in Munich. The pantry was about 8 by 5 feet, a most unlikely place to read a book like the Dissertation. From my perspective now, I would say that if there were one book that captures the essence or wellspring of Edwards's theology, this would be it. Edwards's answer to the question of why God created the world is this: to emanate the fullness of His glory for His people to know, praise, and enjoy. Here is the heart of his theology in his own words:

> IT APPEARS THAT ALL that is ever spoken of in the Scripture as an ultimate end of God's works is included in that one phrase, *the glory of God.* In the creatures' knowing, esteeming, loving, rejoicing in and praising God, the glory of God is both exhibited and acknowledged; his fullness is received and returned. Here is both the *emanation* and *remanation.* The refulgence shines upon and into the creature, and is reflected back to the luminary. The beams of glory come from God, and are something of God and are refunded back again to their original. So that the whole is *of* God and *in* God, and *to* God, and God is the beginning, middle and end in this affair.

That is the heart and center of Jonathan Edwards and, I believe, of the Bible too. That kind of reading can turn a pantry into a vestibule of heaven.

I am not the only person for whom Edwards continues to be a vestibule of heaven. I hear testimonies regularly that people have stumbled upon this man's work and had their world turned upside down. There are simply not many writers today whose mind and heart are God-entranced the way Edwards was. Again and again, to this very day his writings help me know that experience.

My prayer for *The Essential Edwards Collection* is that it will draw more people into the sway of Edwards's God-entranced worldview. I hope that many who start here, or continue here, will make their way to Edwards himself. Amazingly, almost everything he wrote is available on the Internet. And increasingly his works are available in affordable books. I am thankful that Owen Strachan and Douglas Sweeney share my conviction that every effort to point to Edwards, and through him to his God, is a worthy investment of our lives. May that be the outcome of these volumes.

> John Piper
> Pastor for Preaching and Vision
> Bethlehem Baptist Church
> Minneapolis, Minnesota

Jonathan Edwards, Lover of God

*J*onathan Edwards stands tall in America's historical memory and the history of the church. There is little agreement, though, on who he really was.

To some, Edwards was a great philosopher. In the opinion of several notable historians, Edwards represents the greatest philosophical thinker America has produced. On questions that most of us struggle to even comprehend, the New England mastermind provided answers still considered influential today.

To others, Edwards was a great preacher. Mulling over the truths of the Word for days at a time, Edwards wrote sermons that stand as some of the most powerful ever produced. For this group, Edwards is noteworthy primarily as a minister of the Word, one who modeled biblical faithfulness and who saw seasons of incredible blessing fall upon His ministry.

Still others home in on Edwards as a great theologian. They argue that Edwards should be known most for his work to sharpen Christian understanding of the great doctrines of the faith: salvation, holiness, the afterlife, among others.

The multi-dimensionality of Edwards is apparent, and can also include Edwards's status as a college president, the founder of a family dynasty, a husband, and a mentor. Jonathan Edwards was a complex and gifted person, one who defies easy characterization.

With all of these roles, and because of His solemn bearing, Jonathan Edwards intimidates us, to put it plainly. We recall scraps of his writing from high school English classes, and remember vaguely threats of damnation and complex language that was hard to understand. Knowing how deep he went, we shy away from Edwards, aware that we can't play in his league. At a fundamental level, we feel he's just not like us.

Jonathan Edwards was a combination of many rare gifts. But all of these flowed out of one simple and essential reality: Jonathan Edwards was a Christian. He was a believer who followed Jesus Christ in repentant faith. He loved God, and He sought to live for Him. In this fundamental way, Jonathan Edwards was just like you and me.

In this book, we present Edwards's life and thought in short, accessible chapters illustrated by Edwards's sermons and writings. It may take a little time to get used to his style, but it is our belief that investing even a little effort in reading his original writings will yield a bountiful spiritual payoff. His meditations are so deep, so thoughtful, and so fresh that we are confident you will profit from them if you give them a chance. We will splice in our commentary as we sketch a general picture of his life, and we will offer brief suggestions for application from his life and teaching that we hope will be of use to you in your personal reading or in the context of group study.

Though we both relish academic history and love working exhaustively with Edwards and his writings, we do not try to cover every base in this book. In a text of this size, we cannot, though the additional volumes of the *Essential Edwards Collection* allow the reader to delve much deeper into his thinking and preaching. We seek in *Jonathan Edwards: Lover of God* to make Edwards accessible, knowing that if we can succeed in that quest, readers of a wide range of backgrounds—whether those who find him intimidating, those who have never heard of him, or those whose t-shirts identify him as a "homeboy"—will experience the joy of deepened theology and enlivened spirituality. This book is intended for the uninitiated, but we hope and intend for it—and this series—to be of use to pastors, students, church leaders, small groups, and many more besides.

As we head into the text, forget what you may fear about Edwards. Cast aside your doubt; don't worry about boredom. We promise that the story of Edwards's life will richly reward you as you read it. It is not always a happy story—there is hardship along the way, and we will see that Edwards was a human being with flaws and struggles, just like us. But as we go, we will begin to understand the secret of Jonathan Edwards's life. We will gain a desire to live for God in a personally transforming way, a way that, like Edwards, causes us to use our own God-given gifts for the salvation of sinners, the strengthening of God's church, and the glory of our great God. Spanning the centuries and speaking to all Christians, Edwards's example reaches out to us and calls us to taste and see that the Lord is good.

CHAPTER 1

A Happy Beginning

*T*he man who would stand tall in history began life in a minister's home in East Windsor, Connecticut, a small town on the east side of the Connecticut River and the central north of the state. The date was October 5, 1703. Jonathan was the fifth child born to the Rev. Timothy Edwards and Esther Stoddard Edwards. Timothy was a gifted pastor and a good father to his family. He took a special interest in Jonathan, for the two of them formed the entirety of the family's male contingent. Jonathan had no less than ten sisters with whom he got along well. Between the busy life of a New England pastor and the bustle of a crowded home, the family led a full and happy life.

Jonathan's parents were devoted Christians. His father was a well-respected minister and his mother's father, Solomon Stoddard, was a pastor in Northampton, Massachusetts and one of the eminent figures of the Connecticut River Valley. It is hard to picture today, but in colonial New England some three centuries ago, pastors were the leaders of society. Unlike the current day, when the work of the pastor enjoys little respect in society, these clergy possessed significant cultural influence, watched over churches that included most members of a given town, and understood the pastorate as a sacred calling.

Though they related to their people in various ways, they were not primarily administrators, folksy storytellers, or isolated intellectuals. They perceived themselves to be shepherds over God's flock, those who were responsible for the survival and flourishing of God's people. Preaching constituted the means by which such nourishment flowed from God to people, as did careful church oversight involving church discipline and observation of the sacred ordinances (baptism and the Lord's supper). With such a spiritual diet, the colonists of New England were equipped to live in a hard world of taxing labor, frequent sickness, and early death.

In a society that highly respected preachers and that called them to a high standard, Solomon Stoddard was a titan. His congregation was huge, he was a theological authority, and he possessed the bearing of a statesman. To say that Jonathan was born in the line of preachers, then, is no small claim. More accurately, he was born into New England royalty, and he was expected from a young age to pursue the Lord, the ministry, and the application of his considerable gifts in his life's work. He was raised in the church, and he was trained to view it as the theater of the supernatural, the arena in which God's glory shone through the proclaimed Word and the poured-out Spirit. The pastor was at the center of this divine drama. To the perceptive young mind of Jonathan Edwards, his father possessed the ability as a minister to move his people and draw them close to the Lord through preaching. Visits to Grandfather's church in Northampton would only have magnified such an observation as the little boy observed the gathering of hundreds on a weekly basis for worship under Stoddard's magisterial direction.

Young Jonathan's Seriousness

Between the boy's natural gifts and his impressive lineage, it seemed clear to many that young Jonathan had a date with a pastoral destiny in the near future. In time, and with much training, he would meet his destiny, and take the office of colonial pastor to a height unknown by either father or grandfather. He would not do so, however, without considerable preparation for his future ministry. In colonial America, this meant academic study from an early age—six in Jonathan's case. At an age when children today barely know the alphabet, Jonathan began the study of Latin under the tutelage of his father, who supplemented his pastoral income by tutoring boys preparing for college. Jonathan mastered Latin and progressed to Greek and Hebrew by age twelve. His intellectual ability was matched by his irrepressible spiritual fire. He later reflected that in this period:

> I, WITH SOME OF MY SCHOOLMATES joined together, and built a booth in a swamp, in a very secret and retired place, for a place of prayer. And besides, I had particular secret places of my own in the woods, where I used to retire by myself; and used to be from time to time much affected. (*Works* 16, 791)

Though Jonathan had not at this time cried out for salvation, he was clearly engaged in religious activity, activity no doubt prompted by the example of his godly parents. At this point in his life, however, Christianity was more an exercise to be performed than a faith to be experienced. Though he did speak of emotional stirrings when spiritually engaged, it seems that a true work of grace had not yet inhabited his heart and saved his soul. The young Edwards was quite serious about Christianity but had not yet tasted the miracle of conversion.

Jonathan's seriousness extended into areas that were ignored by others of his age. Well before he wrote his famous sermon "Sinners in the Hands of an Angry God," he showed an early sensitivity to the reality of death. In a cheerful letter to his sister Mary, written in 1716 when just twelve, Jonathan reported that:

> THERE HAS FIVE PERSONS DIED in this place since you
> have been gone . . . Goodwife Rockwell, old Goodwife
> Grant, and Benjamin Bancroft, who was drowned in a boat
> many rods from shore, wherein were four young women
> and many others of the other sex, which were very remark-
> ably saved, and the two others which died I suppose you
> have heard of. (*Works* 16, 29)

Residents of colonial New England were more accustomed
to the frequency of death than we are today. Yet we glimpse a
particular awareness of the realm beyond this one in
Jonathan's letter. His tone is not dark or foreboding, but he
clearly understands the nearness of death. Raised by his father
and mother to acknowledge and confront hard realities,
Jonathan was able from a young age to look deeper and clearer
into his world than peers who sought simply to pass the time.

The Scholarly Life Begins

When the time came to attend university, the natural
choice was the Connecticut Collegiate School, known to us
today as Yale University, located in New Haven, some 54 miles
from East Windsor. In 1716, when Jonathan entered a branch
of the school in Wethersfield, his class consisted of twelve
other young men. The teacher was his cousin, Elisha Williams.
The course consisted mainly of reading, memorization, written work, and recitations, in contrast to the contemporary

classroom. The emphasis in the 1700s was more on rote learning and recital than on discussion and lecture. The course of study could be grueling, and students spent many hours in small rooms and hard chairs memorizing their texts.

Jonathan's capacity for logical thought, clear writing, and sharp analysis of an argument developed during this time. In Wethersfield and later New Haven, the young Edwards also indulged his great appetite for theology during his years at Yale, reading classics such as the Puritan William Ames's *The Marrow of Theology*, and other texts that shaped his thinking.

Jonathan's four years at Yale were full of hard work and contemplative intellectual formation. Reading, reflection, and writing would be a part of his life for the remainder of his days. Though a young man with few responsibilities, he devoted himself to the cultivation of his mind. "I am sensible of the preciousness of my time," he wrote his father in 1719, "and am resolved it shall not be through any neglect of mine, if it slips through without the greatest advantage" (*Works* 16, 32). His devotion paid off in September 1720, at the end of his bachelor's degree, when Jonathan graduated as the valedictorian of his class. He delivered a valedictory address in Latin and prepared himself for the next phase of his education, a master's degree, then the highest academic degree attainable.

Jonathan was now a man. In his young life, he had accomplished much and impressed many. He had charted an excellent course for himself and had honored his parents and tutors. Yet he had not tasted the beauty of living for God in repentant, joyful trust. His life was full and good, his mind was sharp, but the dawn was yet to break. In coming days, a strange and wonderful light would shine in Jonathan's heart, transforming a young, scholarly, religious student into a God-intoxicated man.

Applying Edwards's Life and Ideas

A Well-Led Home

Jonathan Edwards's full and happy life did not come out of a vacuum. He grew up in a home that cultivated faith, just as a gardener cultivates healthy plants. He was raised in a home that was devoted to the Lord through the leadership of his father and mother. With the help of his wife, Jonathan's father trained his children to embrace the realities of life in a fallen world and to prepare their souls for the world beyond. When the husband exercises spiritual leadership in this way, and works together with his wife to raise his children in Christian faith, his children will learn to confront hard truths, to take spiritual things seriously, and to pursue the Lord with passion. Though this spiritual preparation might seem unimportant compared to other things, it is in fact the greatest gift that parents can provide their children.

The Importance of Worship to the Family

*T*he Edwards family made worship a fundamental priority. Though not all fathers are pastors like Timothy, all dads can lead their families in worship. Parents can set a pattern for their children in which worship is not an obligation or a chore, but an exciting, life-transforming privilege. The church of God would greatly benefit today from parents that celebrate worship and church involvement like Timothy and Esther Edwards did.

Prioritizing Education

*L*ike the Edwardses, our parenting should also give priority to the educational formation of our children. This will involve emphasizing the importance of a Christian worldview that prizes the life of the mind and that embraces diligent study of numerous fields. No matter what our children go on to do in life, they can honor the Lord by approaching learning with discipline and passion. Enthusiastic parental support for education from an early age will set them on a course to do so.

CHAPTER 2

The Joys of New Birth

*A*fter earning his bachelor's degree, seventeen-year-old Jonathan Edwards plunged into his master's degree. Though he wanted to go into the ministry, he was too young to be a pastor, and he thought it wise to cultivate his mind. Edwards's further preparation set him up to be a pastor who could handle the difficult intellectual challenges of his day. This approach was common in the 1700s, as future pastors sought rigorous preparation for the demands of pastoral ministry. If they were to be leaders of church and society, authorities on a wide variety of fields, able teachers of the Word, they needed excellent preparation. The pastor-theologians, as they are called, sensed the high calling of the pastorate and shaped themselves accordingly. Thus for Jonathan the master's degree was an essential step in preparing for God's work.

"Wrapt Up to God in Heaven": Conversion

In his master's work, Jonathan found that he had more time to mull over the Bible he was studying. Always a contemplative person, he enjoyed meditating on Scripture. One day in the spring of 1721, Edwards pondered 1 Timothy 1:17 (KJV): "Now unto the King eternal, immortal, invisible, the only wise God, be honor and glory for ever and ever. Amen." In the course of this spiritual exercise, one of thousands experienced in his life to this point, something happened. While silently walking along, a thunderclap struck in Jonathan's heart. He later said of that instance:

> AS I READ THE WORDS, there came into my soul, and as it were diffused through it, a sense of the glory of the divine being; a new sense, quite different from anything I ever experienced before. Never any words of Scripture seemed to me as these words did. I thought with myself, how excellent a Being that was; and how happy I should be, if I might enjoy that God, and be wrapt up to God in heaven, and be as it were swallowed up in him. (*Works* 16, 792–3)

This sensation of being "swallowed up" in God erupted into a fresh love for Jesus Christ:

> FROM ABOUT THAT TIME, I began to have a new kind of apprehension and ideas of Christ, and the work of redemption, and the glorious way of salvation by him. I had an inward, sweet sense of these things, that at times came into my heart; and my soul was led away in pleasant views and contemplations of them. And my mind was greatly engaged, to spend my time in reading and meditating on Christ; and the beauty and excellency of his person, and the lovely way of salvation, by free grace in him. (*Works*, 16, 793)

Though he never formally said it, this was Jonathan's conversion experience. He had grown up with Scripture and had been studying it academically for years. He knew it very well and attempted to obey its moral and spiritual guidelines. As important as knowledge and obedience are, neither can save the soul and transform the heart. One must acquire what Jonathan later called the "true sense" of God for conversion to take place:

> A TRUE SENSE OF THE DIVINE and superlative excellency of the things of religion; a real sense of the excellency of God and Jesus Christ, and of the work of redemption, and the ways and works of God revealed in the gospel. There is a divine and superlative glory in these things; an excellency

that is of a vastly higher kind, and more sublime nature than in other things; a glory greatly distinguishing them from all that is earthly and temporal. He that is spiritually enlightened truly apprehends and sees it, or has a sense of it. He does not merely rationally believe that God is glorious, but he has a sense of the gloriousness of God in his heart. There is not only a rational belief that God is holy, and that holiness is a good thing, but there is a sense of the loveliness of God's holiness. There is not only a speculatively judging that God is gracious, but a sense how amiable God is upon that account, or a sense of the beauty of this divine attribute. (*Works* 17, 413)

Jonathan attained this "true sense" while he walked the campus of Yale, pondering the first chapter of 1 Timothy. He suddenly realized in a personal way the majesty, excellency, and greatness of Jesus Christ. He became for Edwards the fountain of beauty and the purpose of life. Once 10,000 miles away, now He was near.

Jonathan would never again abstractly study God. From this moment on, he would enjoy Him. He would seek to know the Lord, a journey that involved the full capacity of his mind, his emotions, and his soul. Jonathan's life would not be easy from this point forward, and he sometimes doubted his salvation, but his commitment would never fade.

The Sweetness of Meditation
and the Reality of Heaven

A year passed in Jonathan's life, one filled with academic work and tutoring of undergraduate students at Yale. In the summer of 1722, though immersed in his studies, Jonathan was called by an English Presbyterian congregation in New York City, then housing about ten thousand residents, many of whom engaged in the booming sea trade. He agreed to serve as pastor of the little church, which had divided over its previous pastor. In the course of Edwards's year in New York, the congregation healed its wounds and called the former minister, James Anderson, back to the pulpit.

Though his stay in the city was brief, Jonathan's passion for the Lord only intensified while in New York. He thought much about heaven, and later reflected on his contemplation: "The heaven I desired was a heaven of holiness; to be with God, and to spend my eternity in divine love, and holy communion with Christ. My mind was very much taken up with contemplations on heaven, and the enjoyments of those there; and living there in perfect holiness, humility and love." Jonathan's delight in heaven sometimes overwhelmed him as:

THE INWARD ARDOR OF MY SOUL, seemed to be hindered and pent up, and could not freely flame out as it would. I used often to think, how in heaven, this sweet principle should freely and fully vent and express itself. Heaven appeared to me exceeding delightful as a world of love. It

appeared to me, that all happiness consisted in living in
pure, humble, heavenly, divine love. (*Works* 16, 795–6)

For many Christians, heaven is a matter-of-fact reality, the
logical end to the Christian life. Jonathan, however, sought to
look deeply into the life to come. He knew from Scripture that
heaven was a place of perfect holiness, a "world of love."
Jonathan knew that while unceasing holiness and happiness
prove evasive on this earth, heaven promised the believer
absolute purity and joy. If young Jonathan had a faraway look
on his daily walks by the Hudson River, it was because he was
thinking of another place.

Jonathan knew that heaven was not a fairy tale mystery.
For Jonathan, the unseen mysteries of the faith, including
heaven, were no less real than earthly life. Earthly life was
merely a shadow of that to come. In his quest to live well for
the Lord, the young Christian focused on the realm where He
resided.

Holy Living and the Resolutions of Action

As he pondered weighty matters like heaven, Jonathan
kept a record of his thoughts. Over the course of his life, he
compiled over 1,400 reflections on matters of doctrine, philosophy, Scripture, and other intellectual interests. Called the
"Miscellanies," these reflections feature the young thinker's
perspectives on the apocalypse, the workings of the mind, sci-
ence, and scriptural passages, among many other subjects.

Jonathan also kept a diary at times, recording the activities and key events of his daily life. He loved to study and to think about his life and world. But he was not lost in the clouds. Jonathan excelled at putting his contemplative faith to practice. His deep thinking did not weaken his decision-making and his capacity to act—it fueled it.

At the same time that Jonathan was meditating on heaven, he drew up for himself a list of spiritual "resolutions" by which to live. His resolutions, seventy in number and compiled over several months, laid out definitive ways in which Jonathan could put his passion and theology into practice. The young man who sought to meditate deeply tried with similar zeal to live "holily," as he put it.

The first resolution centered on the glory of God and the duty to reflect it:

> RESOLVED, THAT I WILL DO whatsoever I think to be most to God's glory, and my own good, profit and pleasure, in the whole of my duration, without any consideration of the time, whether new, or never so many myriads of ages hence. Resolved to do whatever I think to be my duty, and most for the good and advantage of mankind in general. (*Works* 15, 795)

Living for God in pursuit of beauty and joy did not mean a leisurely, airy existence. It meant action that resulted in "God's glory" and Jonathan's "own good." Though he certainly practiced his faith in a fallen way, as all Christians do, Jonathan sought to use all his ability to give God all the glory. This meant a fusion of faith, thought, and action all directed to a doxological end.

Jonathan's aims were not rooted in pride, but they were certainly broad. As a young man, he charted a plan for his life. His sixth resolution vowed that he would live with vigor: "Resolved, to live with all my might, while I do live." History often pictures Edwards as a dry scholar. But he was not a weak or wimpy man. He possessed purpose and energy. He lived a spiritually ambitious life marked by purposeful, focused labor. His resolutions, made when he was very young but remembered throughout his life, fueled all of this activity.

The disciplined Christian life was for Jonathan saturated by the gospel. Resolution eighteen made this clear: "Resolved, to live so at all times, as I think is best in my devout frames, and when I have clearest notions of things of the gospel, and another world." If his intellect, or his status, or his spiritual achievements loomed large in his mind, Jonathan knew that his focus would shift. He would live to be admired or to become famous or to be envied. Such ungodly ambitions would drive his decisions and lead him away from the Savior. If he lived with the gospel in view, though, he would remember his depravity and the grace of God. He would center all of his life and activity in honoring his Savior and in living a life reflective of the gospel. Instead of drifting away from the truth, he would stay the course.

Early in his life, Jonathan sought to twist his whole being into a tool in the hands of God. He wanted to constantly grow as a Christian. Resolution number thirty captured this desire: "Resolved, to strive to my utmost every week to be brought higher in religion, and to a higher exercise of grace, than I was the week before" (*Works* 16, 755). Jonathan knew that if he did not pursue the Lord, he would not grow as a believer. Though he set a rigorous pace, he positioned himself to experience the full blessings of life as a Christian. He desired a life that constantly bore spiritual fruit, just as a tree bears physical fruit in seasons of health. Jonathan knew that the Lord would use such a life in this world for significant ends.

In mapping out his resolutions, Jonathan realized before turning twenty what it takes many people a lifetime to discover: living for God matters more than anything else. In order to accomplish this aim, Jonathan mapped out a plan for his life that would shape his brief time on earth. Because he lived in this way, his life drew the favor of God. In time, it lit up colonial New England like a comet in the night.

Applying Edwards's Life and Ideas

Cultivating the Habit of Meditation

*T*he conversion of Jonathan Edwards was prompted by times of deep thought and meditation. As those who seek the salvation of people around us, including our own family members, we must remember that it sometimes takes time for people to grapple with the realities and demands of biblical Christianity. Though we desire the immediate conversion of unbelievers, we need to sow gospel seeds in their lives by challenging them to confront biblical truths. In the case of children, we do well to raise them in homes that are saturated by Scripture. Parents should cultivate the habits of meditation and biblical study in their children. This will be difficult in a culture that prizes instantaneous gratification and constant entertainment. But if we train our children to ponder the Scripture from a young age, we will help them develop habits of contemplation and reflection that can, with the Spirit's blessing, lead to repentance and faith. By the time Jonathan trusted the Lord, he had developed patterns of thought that brought him face-to-face with God and His gospel. Of course, no one can predict what the Holy Spirit will do. We can do our best, though, to train our children to think deeply about God and His Word, just as Jonathan's parents did.

The Power of Meditating on Heaven and God's Truth

*J*onathan often meditated on the reality of heaven. Though the scriptural doctrine of heaven is shrouded in layers of mystery, and we possess little material by which to figure out what life in the new heavens and earth will look like, Jonathan serves as a model for us in his attempt to set his thoughts on his eternal home. Just as Jonathan stoked the passions of his heart by meditating on heaven, so too can Christians today reflect on the wonderful truths of the Christian faith. We may not express ourselves as Jonathan did, and we may not experience the level of emotion that he did, but we all can lift ourselves up out of the doldrums of daily existence by peeking into the realities of the gospel.

As we drive to our job, or work around the home, or go to school, we can memorize a biblical verse and meditate on it. As we turn over scriptural truths in our minds, we will see them in fresh light. The Bible will come to life when we view it as a life-transforming gift from a loving Creator (Psalm 119). The person and work of Jesus Christ will shine with glory when we contemplate the hugeness of our sin problem (Romans 3). Heaven won't be so mysterious, for example, if we think about how God will rule us in perfect love there (Revelation 21–22). If we would take snatches of our day and devote them to reflection as Jonathan did, we would find a deeper and more satisfying walk with Christ that would redeem not only our time, but our hearts and minds.

Heaven Centers Around God

*A*s we do so, we ought to follow Edwards in defining heaven as the throne room of God. Our afterlife, after all, will not consist primarily of what we might naturally want it to possess. Though we sometimes come up with our own definitions of heaven, and think of it primarily as the place where we meet with loved ones, and do really fun things, and escape eternally from pain and sadness, we would do well to follow Jonathan in his recognition that the Bible teaches us that heaven is primarily about God, and worship of Him. For more on adopting a God-centered vision of heaven, see the writings of pastor John Piper, particularly *Desiring God* and *The Pleasures of God*.

Meditation Followed by Action

*O*ne might be worried that if one goes through with all of this meditating, we'll lose our place in the real world—maybe it sounds like we're suggesting that Christians should walk through life on an airy cloud. While that does sound comfortable, we really want to know the quiet satisfaction of thinking on God. But we also hope to encourage a life of practical action. The first, in fact, fuels the second. The more we think about the deep things of the faith, the more we'll love God, and the greater our desire for holiness and spiritual action will be. Just like Jonathan, who drew up his steps for holiness and action in his "Resolutions," we too can set some spiritual goals for ourselves. We don't need to be legalistic about these goals, and we don't even have to write them down. But we could sketch out some scriptural attitudes and actions that we need to cultivate—the fruit of the Spirit, for example (Galatians 5:22–23)—and lay out some guidelines for ourselves by which to develop these attitudes. Doing so is not legalistic; it's wise, and godly, for the authors of Scripture constantly did this in their letters and writings to the people of God. It will help us to remember the sort of life that we seek as a Christian and will turn us away from sin in moments when we feel like we have lost our way.

In sum, we should seek a blend of Edwardsean thought and action. We should not make the mistake of thinking that either category is best or dominant. The Christian life is a balance of study and activity. Jonathan Edwards provided an excellent example of this in his own life. In the current day, we would do well to emulate him.

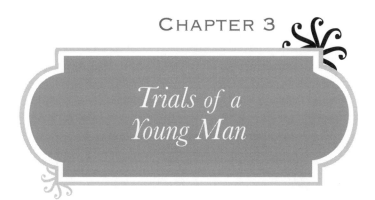

CHAPTER 3

Trials of a Young Man

*J*onathan had pursued high-level academic work for some time before his graduation from his master's program at Yale in September 1723. It was common for students who had attained this honor to deliver a shortened version of their major paper to the campus community at commencement. Jonathan had worked on the matter of individual salvation, specifically on the way that God justifies sinners through faith in His Son. Some in Jonathan's day had questioned the necessity of this central tenet of the Reformation and many disagreed with the young scholar's position. Reading his thesis in Latin, per the academic custom of the day, Jonathan boldly asserted that justification by faith meant that:

GOD RECEIVES THE SINNER into his grace and friendship
for this reason alone, that his entire soul receives Christ in
such a way that righteousness and eternal life are offered in
an absolutely gratuitous fashion and are provided only
because of his reception of Christ. . . . We maintain that
Christ is the complete Savior and not merely the partial
author of our eternal salvation. Because of these consider-
ations we deny that a sinner is his own redeemer and
mediator. (*Works* 14, 61)

Jonathan's master's work placed him squarely in the camp of
orthodox Protestantism. Some in his day challenged the idea
that a sinner had to be saved by divine grace, asserting that
people, in effect, completed their salvation by good works.
Christ had partially achieved redemption through His death,
but needed the obedience of His followers to see them
through to the other side. Jonathan, however, argued with
force that "Christ is the complete Savior," having offered His
perfection to mankind "in an absolutely gratuitous fashion."
Jonathan's study of the Bible had convinced him that God had
to be the initiator and agent of salvation because mankind was
so lost as to be helpless before God. The greatness of God's
power made possible the extent of God's love.

Though he possessed the ability to think for himself, and
to probe doctrines that other people accepted but thought
little about, Jonathan desired from an early age to hold fast to
the tenets of orthodox Christianity. He thought innovatively

(as will be seen in later chapters), and never made himself a slave to tradition, but he never challenged tradition for the sake of doing so. Jonathan searched the Scriptures, learned from his teachers, and strove to be faithful. This frequently meant that he upheld and defended historic views of doctrine. While others of similar abilities chased the latest doctrinal trends, Jonathan displayed from an early age a resolute desire to adhere to what the Bible taught. Though some of his Yale peers and tutors challenged the tradition on the matter of salvation, Jonathan courageously defended the orthodox view. The young Christian showed no allegiance to popular opinion. He was a man of his own mind, and his mind was fundamentally calibrated to stay true to the wisdom of the Word.

In Search of Employment

Soon after graduating from Yale, Jonathan took a preaching assignment in Bolton, Connecticut, near Hartford. After agreeing to settle in the newly formed town, Jonathan found that the church could not support him, either by salary or with a parsonage in which to make his home. Though his father had arranged the call, it fell through. An offer to serve as senior tutor at Yale came soon after. These were hard times for Jonathan. He was well prepared for the work of pastoring and yearned to do it, yet his desire had been frustrated in Bolton. He thus moved back to New Haven for the work of overseeing Yale's forty students in their studies. To one who had just left the college, this seemed a strange providence. But

Jonathan trusted the Lord's will and began his work with zeal.

Sickness of the Body but Not the Soul

Jonathan was a hard-working tutor. He tried diligently to balance the responsibilities of teaching and administration at the small, understaffed college. In the midst of his heavy load, Jonathan ran into a wall that he frequently hit in his adult life. He overworked himself as a young tutor and fell very sick in September 1725. The young tutor had a great deal of mental energy, and wanted to honor his employers, but simply could not because of his sickened body.

Jonathan was not and never would be a physically robust person. He did not pity himself, though. He determined by his strong will to taste the Lord's goodness by applying his mind to the study of God's character. He later wrote of this period that:

IN THIS SICKNESS, God was pleased to visit me with the sweet influences of his spirit. My mind was greatly engaged there on divine, pleasant contemplations, and longings of soul. I observed that those who watched with me, would often be looking out for the morning, and seemed to wish for it. Which brought to my mind those words of the Psalmist, which my soul with sweetness made its own language, "My soul waiteth for the Lord more than they that watch for the morning: I say, more than they that watch for

morning" [Ps. 130:6]. And when the light of the morning
came, and the beams of the sun came in at the windows, it
refreshed my soul from one morning to another. It seemed
to me to be some image of the sweet light of God's glory.
(*Works* 16, 798–9)

In times of difficulty, Jonathan went back to the Lord. He
meditated on Psalm 130 and found refreshment in the Lord
and His sovereignty over Jonathan's life. Jonathan's focus on
the Lord and His goodness enabled him to thrive in his season
of trial. He waited on the Lord, thinking about Him while
huddled in blankets by the fire, seeking to recover his
strength. The days stretched into weeks, and the weeks wore
on, but Jonathan did not need the absence of hardship to
make him happy—only the presence of the Lord.

Though his body struggled for vitality, and his tasks went
undone, Jonathan tasted the beauty of living for God by focusing on God and His goodness as revealed by the psalmist. The
problem of physical weakness would return throughout his
life due to his relentless work ethic and frail constitution.
Despite this challenge, Jonathan tried hard in seasons of difficulty to redeem them and to make them seasons of growth.

The Call of a Lifetime

It took months for Jonathan to recover from his illness.
While healing, an offer came to him to preach in Glastonbury,
a small town close to Hartford. Jonathan preached for several

weeks and once again felt a fire in his bones. His tutoring duties picked back up, however, and his labor in New Haven continued into the summer. The young tutor tired of his vocation, though he plugged away at it until another call came. This one would alter his course forever.

In 1726, Solomon Stoddard, Jonathan's grandfather, needed a pastoral assistant. The people of Northampton had long known Stoddard as a "river god," one of the most powerful figures of the Connecticut River Valley. Northampton, though holding only around 1,100 residents, was a bustling town featuring homes built close to one another in case of attack. Now in his eighties, Stoddard had labored for decades in the town, winning the respect not only of his congregation but his region. His days as a pastor would soon run their course, a fact that caused the town to seek out Jonathan for the training position. The people of Northampton knew Jonathan well. He had won respect and acclaim throughout the colonies for his intellect, his intense devotion to the Lord, and his promise in light of his familial heritage. In November 1726 the congregation voted him in as assistant to Stoddard. The work was challenging, as the church included hundreds of townsfolk, but Jonathan learned quickly, worked hard, and already had several years of preaching behind him. From 1726 to 1728, he preached once on Sunday and taught once on a weekday. In February 1727, the church ordained Jonathan to the ministry. His grandfather led the service. It must have been a poignant scene for both grandfather and grandson. The precocious young boy who grew up in his grandfather's shadow had become a leader of God's people. The stage was set for Jonathan's future assumption of the Northampton pastorate. Still, he lacked one thing.

The Drama of Young Love

Jonathan loved the life of the mind. He could be bookish and isolated, but he had another side, a side that is easy to ignore in studying his career. Though occupying an eminent ministerial position, Jonathan was just twenty-three at this point in his life. He knew the attraction of the fairer sex, and he sought a spouse. His interest centered on a young New Haven woman named Sarah Pierpont. A pastor's daughter, Sarah had first caught Jonathan's attention when he worked as a tutor at Yale. Though young by today's standards, Sarah exhibited a faith and dignity that drew Jonathan like a moth to a flame. The pen that produced eloquent theological treatises later in life served a different purpose in this period as Jonathan, passionately in love, penned some of his most famous lines when reflecting on Sarah. His romantic musing is worth quoting at length:

THEY SAY THERE IS a young lady in New Haven who is beloved of that almighty Being, who made and rules the world, and that there are certain seasons in which this great Being, in some way or other invisible, comes to her and fills her mind with exceeding sweet delight, and that she hardly cares for anything, except to meditate on him—that she expects after a while to be received up where he is, to be raised up out of the world and caught up into heaven; being assured that he loves her too well to let her remain at a distance from him always. There she is to dwell with him, and to be ravished with his love and delight forever. Therefore, if you present all the world before her, with the richest of its treasures, she disregards it and cares not for it, and is unmindful of any pain or affliction. She has a strange sweetness in her mind, and singular purity in her affections; is most just and conscientious in all her actions; and you could not persuade her to do anything wrong or sinful, if you would give her all the world, lest she should offend this great Being. She is of a wonderful sweetness, calmness and universal benevolence of mind; especially after those seasons in which this great God has manifested himself to her mind. She will sometimes go about from place to place, singing sweetly; and seems to be always of joy and pleasure; and no one knows for what. She loves to be alone, and to wander in the fields and on the mountains, and seems to have someone invisible always conversing with her. (*Works* 16, 789–90)

Like any person, Jonathan could appreciate beauty when he saw it, and he thought that this pastor's daughter was lovely.

One can easily imagine him drifting into romantic contemplation while preparing a lesson at his desk in New Haven or a sermon in Northampton. Her face would come to mind, and for a moment, the abstractions of philosophy or theology were forgotten, lost in a world where a woman of "wonderful sweetness" walked closely with her "great God." Sarah's beauty had tapped the romantic side of Jonathan, but her character and her faith elicited his highest praise. Sarah did not want to live for this world. In Jonathan's idealistic expression, "you could not persuade her to do anything wrong or sinful." Unlike many girls her age, Sarah was not led by her passions. As Jonathan saw her, she possessed "a singular purity in her affections," a love for God that transcended other concerns. In Sarah, Jonathan had found a person like him, one so wrapped up in God that she could not be described without reference to Him.

Though Jonathan's language displays the drama of young love, it also reveals that the love Jonathan felt for Sarah possessed a strongly theological character. Here was a woman "ravished" with God's "love and delight" who loved "to wander in the fields and on the mountains," talking with God. The poetry of the passage provides a way to understand how Jonathan and Sarah found one another. Each of these young Christians walked in their own world, devoting themselves to the Lord. When they met and fell for one another, it was as if they met in distant fields that no one else could see. They soon discovered that the path they walked was the same.

Married Life Begins

On July 28, 1727, the spiritual companionship between Jonathan and Sarah took shape in a marriage ceremony in New Haven. After the celebration, the couple traveled to Northampton, where they settled in a parsonage in the heart of the little town. Jonathan led a busy life, often spending over twelve hours of the day in his study, and Sarah busied herself with a wide variety of economic and domestic responsibilities. By all accounts the couple enjoyed much happiness and closeness. For his part, Jonathan was established in his pastoral work and the head of a happy home. His grooming for this ministry was complete. As his grandfather ailed, Jonathan grew stronger. He burned to preach the Word of God to the people of God. The call to the pulpit approached. His life's consuming work would soon begin.

Applying Edwards's Life and Ideas

The Duty of Courage

*J*onathan's courageous defense of justification by faith alone challenges Christians of the current day to contend for biblical truth. In the case of his Yale address, Jonathan actually opposed fellow Christians. Chapter five will show how Jonathan pursued correct doctrine for the health of his flock and the evangelization of the lost. In this chapter, though, we see that Jonathan publicly opposed false doctrine that Christians might not fall into error. His master's address, then, was not a sermon for his people, but a tract for doctrinal faithfulness. It defined the boundaries of Christian orthodoxy for the colonial churches. Jonathan set an example for believers of his day and of those to come in defending the faith. Where cardinal doctrines of the faith suffer attack, and Christians begin to lose sight of their doctrinal foundation, believers must respond. As Paul instructed in his letter to Timothy, his young apprentice: "By the Holy Spirit who dwells within us, guard the good deposit entrusted to you" (2 Timothy 1:14). In the current day, Christians must "guard" the "deposit" of biblical faith just as Timothy did centuries ago.

Staying Faithful and Flexible

*J*onathan's example further encourages us not to pursue doctrinal innovation for its own sake. Edwards was no slave to tradition, but he did not appreciate doctrine merely because it was new. The history of the church bears out that innovation often attracts a crowd. When theologians or pastors propose new doctrines, we should carefully consider them according to Scripture before we adopt them. God does bring fresh illumination into His church at various times, through different voices, but so too does the enemy seek to destroy the faith of the people of God through heresy. If we keep this in mind as we encounter new theological ideas, we will spare ourselves the fate of so many past Christians who began well but eventually drifted away from the truth due to heresy, immaturity, and the inability to distinguish truth from fiction.

The Passion of the Redeemed Heart

Historians and college students often conceive of Jonathan Edwards as a dour, grim-faced theologian who cared for little except thunderous preaching that left people quaking in their boots. In reality, Jonathan was a passionate, tender man who in early manhood yearned with all his being for a wife. When beautiful Sarah first caught his eye, Jonathan fell under a spell. In his deep mind, theology had to share space with romance. His experience corrects our understanding of him and encourages us to seize the good things of life and enjoy them. Contrary to what we might think, Jonathan lived a deeply vigorous and emotional existence in which he embraced the powerful feelings and joys of life. He sought them out, and when they came, he did not shy away from them but breathed them in like air from the ocean. In our day, we should do the same. We should not simply *know* the faith and its inherent goodness, but *taste* it. We should not shy away from emotion, passion, or joy, but should celebrate these things as gifts from God that keep us from being automatons.

This applies to romance as much as anything else. In a world gone mad with lust and the desire for transcendent experience, Christians should be clear that we do not advocate an ascetic, joyless existence, but that we in fact have found the most pleasurable pursuit of them all. Becoming a Christian does not kill delight; it intensifies it. As some have said it, we should out-live the world, displaying the transformative reality of the gospel in the way we work, study, eat, and love.

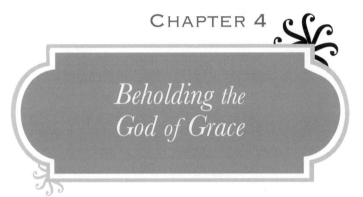

CHAPTER 4

Beholding the
God of Grace

*I*n 1727 Northampton and surrounding towns felt the earth move beneath them. An earthquake struck the New England colonies, shocking residents who had heard of such phenomena but rarely experienced them, and sparking some measure of revival in the area. On February 11, 1729, the town felt a different kind of tremor when Solomon Stoddard, the "pope" of the surrounding country, passed away. Two days later, the church memorialized Stoddard in a burial service. Leaving little place for sentimentality, Jonathan preached a sermon in Stoddard's honor entitled "Living Unconverted under an Eminent Means of Grace." He exhorted his hearers to repent of their sins, no matter how long they had been a member of the Northampton church. In this initial move, Jonathan took the helm of the congregation with a firm grip, setting the tone for his ministry that characterized it until its end.

Strenuous Labor, Humbling Results

Jonathan worked very hard as a young head pastor, leading him to collapse in a matter of months. Throughout the spring of 1729, Jonathan stayed at home. He had again driven himself with such passion that he damaged his health. If the young pastor's sense of urgency allowed him to accomplish much, it also drove him into the ground and hindered his ministry. If this would seem like the error of a young man, Jonathan repeated this mistake throughout his life. In the midst of this self-inflicted trial, Jonathan celebrated his second anniversary and the first birthday of his child, Sarah. She was the first, but not the last. Ten more would eventually join the family.

Exalting Divine Grace

Between 1730 and 1734, the year a great revival broke out in Northampton, the Edwards family enjoyed several relatively quiet years. Jonathan devoted himself to the craft of sermonizing, the care of his congregation, and the cultivation of his young and thriving family. The intensity that occasionally drove Jonathan to exhaustion aided in the production of masterful sermons whose fame soon spread throughout the colonies. Spending thirteen hours daily in the study gave the preacher a substantial block of time with which to work. Because Jonathan concentrated by the minute, and did not whittle his time away in idle pursuits, he was able to compose sermons of great insight and spiritual benefit. In one of his most famous sermons from this period, "God Glorified in Man's Dependence," preached in July 1731, Edwards outlined the dimensions of divine grace, observing that:

THE REDEEMED HAVE ALL from the grace of God. It was of mere grace that God gave us his only begotten Son. The grace is great in proportion to the excellency of what is given. The gift was infinitely precious, because it was of a person infinitely worthy, a person of infinite glory; and also because it was of a person infinitely near and dear to God. The grace is great in proportion to the benefit He have given us in him. The benefit is doubly infinite, in that in him we have deliverance from an infinite, because an eternal, misery, and do also receive eternal joy and glory. The grace in bestowing this gift is great in proportion to our unworthiness to whom it is given; instead of deserving such a gift, we merited infinitely ill of God's hands. The grace is great according to the manner of giving, or in proportion to the humiliation and expense of the method and means by which a way is made for our having the gift. He gave him to dwell amongst us; he gave him to us incarnate, or in our nature; and in the like through sinless infirmities. He gave him to us in a low and afflicted state; and not only so, but as slain, that he might be a feast for our souls. (*Works* 17, 203)

One finds in these poetic words of Edwards a passion to communicate the dimensions of God's grace. Jonathan used the repetition of words—"infinitely" and "infinite" occur six times in close proximity—to drive home a particular concept in his hearer's minds. Here, he sought to stretch his congregation's understanding of grace. As the fiery preacher saw it, many in his day made too little of grace. In focusing heavily on what a person's will could accomplish, one ended up cheapening the power of divine grace. As Jonathan conceived of grace given by God, however, it was, like its source, awesome. Where some might have pictured it as a sweet and gentle stream from which to drink as one saw fit, Jonathan saw God's grace as a tide of goodness that overwhelmed the sinner. God, if He were truly divine, could not be small; grace, if it were truly grace, could not be weak.

God as the End of All Things

God was the source of grace. In Jonathan's mind, though, He was not a means to an end. He *was* the end. In conversion, one did not profess faith in God and then move on. As Jonathan understood Him, God was a sovereign, a mighty ruler, a figure too glorious to take in, even by eyes of faith.

Those who met God in salvation, then, did not move on to better things after their conversion. In their new birth, they had found the Lord of the universe and the goodness they had always sought, as shown in another elegant section of "God Glorified":

GOD HIMSELF IS THE GREAT GOOD which they are brought to the possession and enjoyment of by redemption. He is the highest good, and the sum of all that good which Christ purchased. God is the inheritance of the saints; he is the portion of their souls. God is their wealth and treasure, their food, their life, their dwellingplace, their ornament and diadem, and their everlasting honour and glory. They have none in heaven but God; he is the great good which the redeemed are received to at death, and which they are to rise to at the end of the world. The Lord God is the light of the heavenly Jerusalem; and is the "river of the water of life" that runs, and "the tree of life that grows, in the midst of the paradise of God." The glorious excellencies and beauty of God will be what will for ever entertain the minds of the saints, and the love of God will be their ever-lasting feast. The redeemed will indeed enjoy other things; they will enjoy the angels, and will enjoy one another; but that which they shall enjoy in the angels, or each other, or in any thing else whatsoever that will yield them delight

and happiness, will be what shall be seen of God in them.
(*Works* 17, 208)

The force of Jonathan's speech, with God functioning as the subject of successive sentences, drew the attention of his hearers to the awesomeness of God. Seen through eyes of faith, the Lord is great, and high, and holy. His people feed on His greatness and bask in His transcendence even as they draw comfort from His immanent presence. For Edwards, life is not about one's selfish interests and heaven is not about one's prefabricated paradise. Earthly life and heavenly life alike revolve around the greatness of God.

The Word of Light and Truth

Jonathan discovered the glory of God in a personal way through study of the Word of God. In his famous sermon "A Divine and Supernatural Light," preached in August 1733, Edwards detailed how a person came to understand the beauty of the Bible. When one reads the Scripture with faith:

A TRUE SENSE OF THE DIVINE excellency of the things of God's word doth more directly and immediately convince of the truth of them; and that because the excellency of these things is so superlative. There is a beauty in them that is so divine and godlike, that is greatly and evidently distinguishing of them from things merely human, or that men are the inventors and authors of; a glory that is so high and great, that when clearly seen, commands assent to their divinity and reality. When there is an actual and lively discovery of this beauty and excellency, it will not allow of any such thought as that it is a human work, or the fruit of men's invention. This evidence that they that are spiritually enlightened have of the truth of the things of religion, is a kind of intuitive and immediate evidence. They believe the doctrines of God's word to be divine, because they see divinity in them; i.e., they see a divine, and transcendent, and most evidently distinguishing glory in them; such a glory as, if clearly seen, does not leave room to doubt of their being of God, and not of men. (*Works* 16, 415)

The Bible served as the means by which one could unearth the "beauty and excellency" of the Lord. In reading the teachings and stories of Scripture, one found a "divine and godlike" quality that distanced the sacred text from all other books. The contents of Scripture contained a "distinguishing glory" that marked it as the very Word of God to mankind. Edwards did not see the Bible as a static collection of timeless truths and moral maxims. He viewed the Scripture as a living thing. It pulsed with life; it shone with beauty; it bore the glory of God.

This last facet of Edwards's understanding of Scripture relates directly to the way he lived. Jonathan did not practice a weak faith filled with doubt and worry about the irrationality of belief and the mystery of God. As Jonathan saw it, faith was reasonable—that is, it made sense—and doubt was irrational. The Bible accounted for this confidence. The Spirit had spoken through the Word to Jonathan's heart, performing a surgery of the soul and mind such that Jonathan's synapses fired from a position of faith. As he put it in "A Divine and Supernatural Light," the divine nature of the Word "does not leave room" for doubt. If studied with trust, it reorients a person's world such that one sees that God is fundamentally true and right. As a result, believers can live and speak with great boldness.

"A Divine and Supernatural Light" shows us that Jonathan operated from a position of experiential trust in the Lord. Jonathan had not tamed the Word of God such that he could extract from it what he liked and believe what he preferred. The beauty of God's living Word had captured Jonathan. His convinced mind and captivated heart formed the foundation from which all his exhortation and teaching sprang. The majesty and beauty of God, communicated in His Word, beckoned to all, offering every person the opportunity to experience the transforming power of trust.

Meditation and the
Frustrating Struggle to Mortify Sin

Edwards thought it important to meditate on these truths. He often enjoyed riding and walking in nature, where he would think, pray, and relish the natural beauty of unspoiled New England. One can conjecture that these excursions provided a good deal of the contemplation that fueled the pastor's expansive preaching and teaching. Time in nature meant rest, relaxation, and refreshment. Without such times, it is doubtful that Edwards would have accomplished all that he did or communed as deeply with the Lord as his brief retreats made possible.

Edwards's efforts bore tremendous fruit. The young pastor knew his share of dark days, however. No person can evade faithless thoughts and sinful appetites, no matter how strong their faith may be. Years after Jonathan penned his monumental sermons, he reflected on this period in his life, noting that amidst the highs of spiritual growth, it contained no small amount of struggle with sin:

> OFTEN, SINCE I LIVED IN THIS TOWN, I have had very affecting views of my own sinfulness and vileness; very frequently to such a degree as to hold me in a kind of loud weeping, sometimes for a considerable time together; so that I have often been forced to shut myself up. I have had a vastly greater sense of my own wickedness, and the badness of my heart, than ever I had before my conversion. It has often appeared to me, that if God should mark iniquity against me, I should appear the very worst of all mankind; of all that have been since the beginning of the world to this time; and that I should have by far the lowest place in the world to this time; and that I should have by

far the lowest place in hell. When others, that have come to
talk with me about their soul concerns, have expressed the
sense they have had of their own wickedness by saying,
that it seemed to them, that they were as bad as the devil
himself; I thought their expressions seemed exceeding faint
and feeble, to represent my wickedness. (*Works* 16, 801–2)

Students of Edwards need to mark these words. We should
not view him as a super-Christian. The Northampton pastor
modeled a faithful Christian life of great depth and joy, but he
was a man, and a sinner, just like the rest of the race. This
passage captures this reality. Though Edwards does not spell
out specific sins in which he indulged, he makes clear that
he fought a great fight against his own indwelling sin, a fight
that he sometimes lost.

Whether faced with pride, arrogance, jealousy, self-suffi-
ciency, or other personal weaknesses, Edwards recognized
that the stuff of "vileness" moved in his bones. He preached
great sermons, and he ministered powerfully to his family,
church, and society, but he also hurt his wife, and wronged his
children, and spoke bitterly against his church, just as every
Christian does. He tried to work hard without complaining,
but he surely did; he yearned to stop pride in its tracks, but he
sometimes could not. His days as a pastor in Northampton
brought great blessing and encouragement, but they also
brought struggle, and pain, and the profoundly humbling real-
ization that "if God should mark iniquity" on his account, he
would not stand, but would fall into an eternity of darkness

and destruction from which no person could emerge. As a young pastor, the beauty of living for God mingled with the pain of living in sin. This pain did not overwhelm him, but neither did it leave his side. Jonathan's life was like that of every Christian. It was a struggle, a fight for faith, that did not rest until the end of his life.

Family Leadership

In a difficult period, the natural rhythms of life and family brought Jonathan refuge from despair, as they so often do. From the time they arrived in Northampton, the Edwardses watched as their family steadily grew. Sarah came along in 1728, Jerusha in 1730, and Esther in 1732. In coming years, Mrs. Edwards gave birth to eight more children—Mary (1734), Lucy (1736), Timothy (1738), Susannah (1740), Eunice (1743), Jonathan Jr. (1745), Elizabeth (1747), and Pierrepont (1750). In the midst of a packed calendar, the Edwardses produced nothing less than a tribe. Though families in this era often grew quite large, the Edwards home seems as filled with happiness as it was with children. Jonathan and Sarah each exuded dignity and authority, but they also easily won the affection and loyalty of their children.

As his father had done, Jonathan provided tender spiritual leadership for his children. On the weekends, Edwards catechized his charges, and led them in a special time of singing and prayer on Saturday night in preparation for the spiritual feast of the next day. On weekday mornings, Jonathan read a chapter in the Bible and then commented briefly on the text, according to his protégé Samuel Hopkins. Once the day began, Edwards took up his pen and dove into the life of the mind, writing sermons and treatises and reading books. He frequently interrupted his work, though, for interaction with his children, "to treat with them in his Study, singly and particularly about their . . . Soul's Concerns," always being "careful and thorough in the Government of his Children." In response, his children "reverenced, esteemed and loved him" (Sweeney, Chapter 2, 10). Edwards was not a perfect father, but the record of his family life shows that he did not selfishly shut himself off from his loved ones. As important as his work was to the pastor, it seems that his children took first priority. Their later flowering testifies to this. The girls married well and had numerous children who became Christian leaders and important social figures. The boys distinguished themselves as pillars of their communities and the broader New England region. The lives of successive generations suggest that the Lord blessed the Edwards home for its fidelity to Him.

Applying Edwards's Life and Ideas

Prioritizing Rest and Balance

*I*n a hard-driving world, Christians should mark the way that Jonathan worked himself to debilitation time and again during his career. Some of us, of course, have the opposite tendency, but others struggle just as Jonathan did to approach their work and responsibilities in a balanced way. When one becomes too driven in the area of primary duty, all other areas of life will suffer: family, friends, church involvement, evangelism, and more. It is wise to rest and to pace oneself. Furthermore, it is humble to do so. Though it may not seem to be motivated by pride, overworking sometimes reveals a desire to control the world such that one cannot be happy unless all is in immediate order. Though it seems strange in a very busy age, resting can often glorify the Lord since it expresses humility and a recognition of God's sovereignty. If we would seek to emulate Edwards in his work ethic, we also should seek a more balanced life than he achieved, for the good of ourselves and our families and, ultimately, for the glory of God.

Letting God Be God

*I*n his preaching and teaching, Edwards excelled in allowing
God to be God. Following his example, Christians should
not view God as small or impotent. We should take our con-
ception of the triune God from Scripture and recognize that
God is inherently majestic and worthy of our worship. A large
view of God will lead us to a large view of grace. Rightly
understanding the Lord will lead us to thank Him for His
work in our lives. We can constantly offer prayers of this
nature to God, thanking Him in a sentence or two for conde-
scending to reach us and speak to us in His Word. The act of
revelation, of speaking, is itself an act of grace on the part of
God. We ought to recognize this and approach Scripture with
deeply thankful hearts when we read it throughout the week.
Our view of Scripture must not be small, either, but must
comprehend that the Bible is a living book, a text unlike any
other, which has the power to swallow us whole and transform our lives. As Jonathan did, we must remember these
things and act upon them in our everyday lives. These truths
are not merely nice sermon material. They are the means to a
happy, victorious, God-saturated Christian life.

The Duty to Fight Doubt

A proper understanding of God, one based in the Bible,
will equip the Christian to fight doubt. Satan is an active
agent in our lives, and he will attempt to lead us to doubt God

frequently over the course of our existence as Christians. How essential, then, that like Jonathan we drink deeply from the Word for the purpose of strengthening our faith. The more we hesitate to spend time in Scripture, the more we will struggle to find assurance in moments of doubt. The more we meditate on Scripture, though, the more we will lay hold of firm confidence and dispel doubts when the enemy sends them. Pastor Tim Keller's *The Reason for God* and other apologetics books will buttress our study of the Bible by pointing out reasonable answers to questions about the Christian faith.

With such resources, we can ward off doubt and despair and conform our mind to the Scripture so that it will grow strong and sure (as Romans 12 assures us will happen). This is essential, because Satan will tempt us not only to doubt God intellectually, but also to doubt the progress and existence of our faith. At times, we will feel like Edwards, and wonder if we truly have any faith at all. We will taste the bitterness of sin after we speak unkindly to our spouse, or fail to care for a dear friend, or compromise our ethics at school or work, or gossip about peers, or revel in pride when in the company of people we dislike. We will justly feel shame after such sins, and we must carefully repent of them, but we must also avoid an ungodly sense of melancholy and despair that robs us of effectiveness in the faith.

Finding Joy in Family Life

*T*he rhythms of the family are an excellent antidote to sin for married Christians. Like Edwards, Christian spouses should not shirk their families or retreat from them, but should throw their energy into them, finding release and delight as they cultivate loving relationships with their spouse and children. Though Edwards loved the life of the mind, he also embraced the rhythms of the family and cleared out significant portions of time for his loved ones. Benefit flows both ways when parents invest in their children. Even the busiest among us need the blessing that only loved ones can provide.

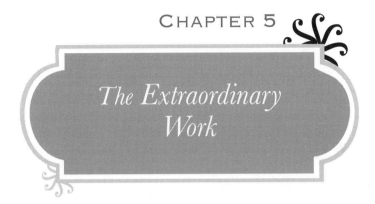

CHAPTER 5

The Extraordinary Work

*T*he early 1730s were a period of calm in the life of the Edwards family. Life was busy, and the family welcomed several children into the world in this period, but Jonathan found large blocks of time to think, write, and care for the needs of his congregation.

In the winter of 1734, everything changed. Jonathan had long preached for revival in his sermons. He sought to draw his people, many of them nominal Christians, to faith in Christ. Suddenly, without warning, the preaching of the young pastor lit a spark. Edwards preached a series of sermons on true Christianity and the scriptural truths that produced it. The series bought a spiritual harvest not seen in Northampton for decades.

This spark spread to a flame, and left little Northampton basking in a spiritual revival. Edwards's pastoral strategy worked to a degree he did not expect and could not have imagined. Soon, Christians from all corners of the world were writing to the thirty-one-year-old pastor, wondering why and how this providence had struck the Massachusetts countryside.

A Narrative of One Town's Salvation

It is worth quoting Edwards at length to reveal the drama of this story. Writing to a friend in Boston in May 1735, Edwards made a number of observations that best summed up the origins of the revival. This letter, later revised into a book, tells a fascinating story of one community's spiritual revival:

IN THE APRIL FOLLOWING, anno 1734, there happened a very sudden and awful death of a young man in the bloom of his youth; who being violently seized with a pleurisy, and taken immediately very delirious, died in about two days; which (together with what was preached publicly on that occasion) much affected many young people. This was followed with another death of a young married woman, who had been considerably exercised in mind, about the salvation of her soul, before she was ill, and was in great distress in the beginning of her illness; but seemed to have satisfying evidences of God's mercy to her, before her death; so that she died very full of comfort, in a most earnest and moving manner warning and counselling others. This seemed to contribute to render solemn the spirits of many young persons; and there began evidently to appear more of a religious concern on people's minds. (*Works* 4, 147–8)

Theological debates also swept through the land in this era, leaving some wondering about their true spiritual state. In this setting, Edwards recounted that:

MANY WHO LOOKED ON THEMSELVES as in a Christless condition, seemed to be awakened by it, with fear that God was about to withdraw from the land, and that we should be given up to heterodoxy and corrupt principles; and that then their opportunity for obtaining salvation would be past; and many who were brought a little to doubt about the truth of the doctrines they had hitherto been taught, seemed to have a kind of trembling fear with their doubts, lest they should be led into bypaths, to their eternal undoing: and they seemed with much concern and engagedness of mind, to inquire what was indeed the way in which they must come to be accepted with God. There were then some things said publicly on that occasion, concerning justification by faith alone. (*Works* 4, 148)

The heightened awareness of death and increased interest in
the person of Christ mingled to produce a great hunger for
God that soon manifested itself in force in Northampton. In
December 1734:

> THE SPIRIT OF GOD BEGAN extraordinarily to set in, and
> wonderfully to work amongst us; and there were, very sud-
> denly, one after another, five or six persons who were to all
> appearance savingly converted, and some of them wrought
> upon in a very remarkable manner.
>
> Particularly, I was surprised with the relation of a
> young woman, who had been one of the greatest com-
> pany-keepers in the whole town. When she came to me, I
> had never heard that she was become in any wise serious,
> but by the conversation I then had with her, it appeared to
> me that what she gave an account of was a glorious work
> of God's infinite power and sovereign grace; and that God
> had given her a new heart, truly broken and sanctified. I
> could not then doubt of it, and have seen much in my
> acquaintance with her since to confirm it. (*Works* 4, 149)

Edwards wondered to himself what this startling conversion
would bring. Would some of this young woman's friends react
to this development by disparaging him and cursing God?
Would they turn their back on the church even more now that
it had taken one of their own? The results proved just the

opposite. In contrast to his fears, the young pastor found that:

> THE EVENT WAS THE REVERSE, to a wonderful degree;
> God made it, I suppose, the greatest occasion of awakening
> to others, of any thing that ever came to pass in the town.
> I have had abundant opportunity to know the effect it had,
> by my private conversation with many. The news of it
> seemed to be almost like a flash of lightning, upon the
> hearts of young people all over the town, and upon many
> others. Those persons amongst us, who used to be farthest
> from seriousness, and that I most feared would make an ill
> improvement of it, seemed to be awakened with it; many
> went to talk with her, concerning what she had met with;
> and what appeared in her seemed to be to the satisfaction
> of all that did so. (*Works* 4, 117)

In the end, the revival exerted a powerful influence on the
people of Northampton. In such a close environment, news of
the revival spread like thunder across the plain. To Edwards's
eyes, the town changed, and became a center of worship:

> THERE WAS SCARCELY A SINGLE PERSON in the town,
> either old or young, that was left unconcerned about the
> great things of the eternal world. Those that were wont to be
> the vainest and loosest, and those that had been most dis-
> posed to think and speak slightly of vital and experimental

religion, were now generally subject to great awakenings. And the work of conversion was carried on in a most astonishing manner, and increased more and more; souls did as it were come by flocks to Jesus Christ. From day to day, for many months together, might be seen evident instances of sinners brought out of darkness into marvel-lous light, and delivered out of an horrible pit, and from the miry clay, and set upon a rock with a new song of praise to God in their mouths [1 Pet. 2:9, Ps. 40:2–3]. (*Works* 4, 150)

From Edwards's account, it appears that something unique and rather extraordinary did occur in Northampton in the mid-1730s. His summary of the revival makes only the briefest mention of the sermonic content that prompted the awakening. This humble omission, however, does obscure the true cause of the event. Edwards had preached a series of lec-tures on justification and the new birth in fall 1734. His preaching to his congregation differed from his earlier trea-tise on justification and salvation that he delivered at Yale in 1723. There, Edwards preached defensively, to contend for the traditional Protestant understanding of justification in a public setting. In 1734, the pastor preached offensively. He wished to clarify the substance of saving faith in Jesus Christ for his congregation so that they might find salvation.

Edwards believed that certain members of his flock had either deceived themselves about their spirituality or had mis-understood the nature of saving faith and the new birth due to unbiblical teaching on the doctrine of justification by faith alone, and he thus set out to win them to a vibrant understanding of this teaching that would nourish Christians and rescue unbelievers.

Edwards maintained that it is faith in Christ alone that:

> JUSTIFIES, OR GIVES AN INTEREST in Christ's satisfaction and merits, and a right to the benefits procured thereby, viz., as it thus makes Christ and the believer one in the acceptance of the Supreme Judge. 'Tis by faith that we have a title to eternal life, because 'tis by faith that we have the Son of God, by whom life is. (*Works* 19, 158)

As articulated here, faith in Christ had the crucial effect of uniting Christ and the believer, once separated by a chasm of sin and unbelief. This was a crucial point. His sermons on justification helped, he thought, "to establish the judgments of many in this truth" and also "to engage their hearts in a more earnest pursuit of justification" (795).

Engage hearts he did. Through these sermons, many unbelievers came to saving faith, leaving the chains of sin and misery behind, and many Christians found fresh assurance of their salvation, leading them to live more joyfully and obediently. There were surely some false conversions and unfulfilled hopes in this season, but the revival that begin in Northampton and swept throughout the Connecticut River Valley in the mid-1730s accomplished much for God's kingdom.

Edwards modeled godly shepherding in his preaching on saving faith. He knew that he was responsible for the spiritual well-being of his people and that this role necessitated that he publicly articulate biblical truth for the health of his people and also for the salvation of some who thought themselves converted. For Edwards, truth and doctrine were not minor matters, mere footnotes of the Christian faith that believers arranged as they saw fit. If he and his fellow ministers tinkered with these truths, Christians would grow weak and worldly. Their minds would grow confused, their hearts weak, and men and women would spiritually suffer even as God lost glory due to Him. If churches held fast to truth, however, and preached it passionately and vigorously, Christians would flourish and stand firm in their faith. They would taste the rich blessings of theological confidence and spiritual hope. Unbelievers would see this distinctive way of life and question their beliefs and behaviors. Though embattled, the church and its members would remain faithful and fruitful. God, observing and orchestrating these events from His throne, would gain glory.

Doctrine as a Means to Joy

Edwards yearned to produce true Christians in his town and to see the faith of those Christians flourish and multiply. He preached and prayed and exhorted toward this end. He did not seek to change the emotions of his flock, nor did he wish merely to equip his people to win theological arguments or memorize a body of doctrine. Edwards labored to communicate truth to his people so that their souls might brim with passion and love for God. Doctrine, then, was a means to love, the factory of passion, the genesis of joy. The Lord rewarded this emphasis. He placed His hand on the little town and its neighbors, marking it for the ages as an example of what the Word moving through a church can accomplish when the Spirit moves with it in a mighty way.

The Revival Declines

The revival soon waned in intensity, though Edwards observed positive effects of his preaching throughout the late-1730s. However, in March 1737, a catastrophe struck the Northampton church. During a service, the decrepit church gallery collapsed, causing people sitting on the second floor to land on the people in the pews below. Somehow, none of the parishioners lost their lives in the accident, and the church resolved to redouble efforts to build a new meeting house. These plans, which had languished for some time, led to the dedication of a new building on Christmas Day of December 1737.

The order of seating in the new building caused Edwards some discomfort, however, as the building's designers had arranged the pews according to the accumulated wealth of their patrons. Jonathan grew quite angry over this and voiced his displeasure to the church, though his denunciations achieved little. This pattern would repeat itself numerous times in the coming years, with the intensity of dialogue soon reaching a pitch that only separation would quiet. Jonathan possessed impressive powers of articulation, but he sometimes struggled with matters of personal communication and tended on occasion to speak harshly when a gentler tone would have sufficed. Like many of us, Edwards's strengths were also his weaknesses. His ability to nuance an argument and state it with great authority helped to persuade many readers of the soundness of his writings. Yet these same qualities sometimes escalated congregational debates that were unworthy of the proportions they reached. Further displeasure resulted from the suicide of Edwards's uncle and church communicant, Joseph Hawley, in 1735, and from the excommunication of a church member, Abigail Bridgman, for drunkenness in July 1739. The exhilaration of 1734 seemed to have given way to frustration and disappointment in the latter half of the 1730s and the early months of 1740.

Whitefield Pays a Visit

The clouds lifted when the young evangelist George Whitefield touched down in Northampton. The young Whitefield was a natural force for the gospel. He preached with a power few of his era could claim. He had it all—eloquence, a booming baritone, passionate piety, scriptural knowledge, and a deep sense of the drama of the gospel. Whitefield had preached to tens of thousands by this time, though he was only twenty-six years old. Hundreds of people from America and England had responded to his call to conversion, making Whitefield the first trans-Atlantic celebrity. In this era, when religion ruled the roost, a wildly successful evangelist like Whitefield routinely stole the headlines of local newspapers. For his part, Whitefield did not oppose such publicity. A talented publicist, he embraced media coverage of his evangelism, and sought to use it to push the gospel even further into the consciences of colonial citizens.

Whitefield employed his capacity for organization by contacting Edwards on his second trip to the colonies in 1740. Though Edwards was young and had not published a great deal at this point, he already had a reputation as a leading pastor and promoter of revival in his region. Whitefield desired permission to preach at Edwards's church. Edwards responded warmly to Whitefield: "I have a great desire, if it may be the will of God, that such a blessing as attends your person and labors may descend on this town, and may enter mine own house, and that I may receive it in my own soul" (*Works* 16, 80). Edwards knew that such a visit could bring with it powerful results and declared his excitement openly to Whitefield: "I hope this is the dawning of a day of God's mighty power and glorious grace to the world of mankind." The expectation of Whitefield's visit gave Edwards hope that revival would visit Northampton once more.

The eminent ministers met on October 17–19, 1740, in Northampton. Whitefield preached movingly in four separate sermons, affecting the congregation in visible ways. Even stoic Jonathan could not contain tears of joy upon hearing the gospel of Christ proclaimed with such electric feeling. The two men enjoyed fellowship during Whitefield's stay in the Edwards home and forged a lasting friendship. Edwards went so far as to rebuke Whitefield after hearing the young, passionate speaker denounce certain colonial pastors for lack of emotion and zeal for the gospel. Though Edwards shared his friend's concerns, he sought to refine Whitefield's public method. He succeeded in doing so, a testimony to the evangelist's respect for the preacher.

The Fruits of Whitefield's Preaching

In later months, Edwards wrote to his friend, giving him a report of the results of Whitefield's visit to Northampton. "I have reason to think that a considerable number of young people, some of them children, have already been savingly brought home to Christ. I hope salvation has come to this house since you was in it, with respect to one, if not more, of my children" (*Works* 16, 87). Edwards then shared a desire to know a similar anointing on his own ministry. Pray for me, he said, "that I may become fervent, as a flame of fire in my work, and may be abundantly succeeded, and that it would please God, however unworthy I am, to improve me as an instrument of his glory, and advancing the kingdom of Christ."

In the visit of the young evangelist, Edwards had glimpsed a life stamped by zeal for the gospel. George Whitefield worked tirelessly to advance the message of salvation, retiring late to bed and rising early in the morning in order to talk with as many people as he could. Even after leading many to the Savior, Jonathan Edwards desired to grow as an evangelist. In his mind, he had not "arrived" as a faithful Christian. He knew that he would never perfectly consecrate himself to his ministry. Yet he pressed on toward the high calling of faith, working hard to bolster his preaching and his Christian witness. His efforts would soon pay off—in even more dramatic fashion than the earlier revival. As his letter indicated, after Whitefield's visit, Edwards freshly committed himself to communicating the glory and drama of the gospel to his people in his weekly sermons. As he did so, his preaching reached greater heights. Many more townspeople experienced the new birth. The Great Awakening, begun several years earlier, soon reached its peak as the words of the Northampton pastor gripped his congregation with a force only divine unction can account for.

Applying Edwards's Life and Ideas

Humility Rather than Jealousy

*I*f a Christian today can take any "secret" from this period of Edwards's life, it is this: to pursue in a simple but concerted way increased conformity of the heart and mind *to* Christ for the purpose of increased spiritual harvest *for* Christ. Edwards demonstrated no jealousy or competitiveness with Whitefield, sins into which he could easily have fallen due to Whitefield's success as an evangelist. Instead, Edwards seems to have been sharpened and encouraged by Whitefield's example. Sadly, Christian friendship often faces the challenge of jealousy, a sin that Christians rarely talk openly about. For his part, Edwards seems to have avoided jealousy over Whitefield's ministry. We are reminded of the need to fight jealousy in our own lives, particularly in matters that we care about. It is one thing to feel little jealousy over things that do not matter to us; it is quite another to demonstrate humility when others have precisely what we desire.

Relentless Pursuit of the Lord

*S*imilarly, like Edwards, we must never think that we have arrived as wholly mature Christians. We must always read and listen to good sermons and talk freely and humbly with others for the purpose of growing in grace. Too many Christians reach a certain level of maturity and then content themselves with a faith that merely coasts through life. The problem with such an approach is that one can only coast so long. When challenges come, one has to pedal strongly to survive, let alone thrive. Indeed, trials can sometimes last a very long time—even a lifetime. If one is truly converted but has spent little time building up the muscles of faith, one will greatly struggle when life's difficulties visit. Like Edwards, who strove to build up his faith in good seasons and bad, Christians should train themselves to engage in a humble but dogged pursuit of the Lord, never settling for a static level of maturity when a higher one is attainable. If athletes push for an earthly prize, one that fades and is forgotten in a matter of years, how much more should we pursue the Lord, whose rewards will not spoil or corrupt but will satisfy the soul into all eternity?

This kind of lifestyle will not happen by accident. Jonathan strove to be a faithful and fruitful Christian in his daily life through regular and sustained study of the Scriptures and prayer. He tried to give himself power for godly living through his devotional life. He armed himself with Scripture and doctrinal study to train his mind and offered up fervent prayers for the mortification of his sin. The pastor tried constantly to grow closer to God. He yearned to be even more fruitful than he was. His prayer for an invigorated ministry reflects these desires.

This pattern of godly living provides modern-day Christians with an excellent example to emulate. Jonathan struggled with pride, as we all do, but he strove to walk humbly before God and man. He was no perfect man, but he constantly recommitted himself to the pursuit of godliness. Whatever our calling, whatever our station in life, we should do the same.

Toward a "Missional" Faith

*T*he way in which Edwards sought the revival of his church and the salvation of the lost ought to receive attention from Christians today. With an eighteenth-century perspective, Edwards worked to fulfill the Great Commission in his own life and pastorate. It is not necessary to adopt a certain model or method in order to advance the gospel in this world, but it is necessary that churches—and the individual Christians who compose them—see themselves as agents of Christ for the spread of the gospel. This means adopting what some call a "missional" mindset, but may also be called more traditionally an "evangelistic" way of life. Such a lifestyle will naturally look different than it would have in the 1730s, but believers today can proclaim the gospel just as Edwards did in his generation.

Through conversations and meals with neighbors, discussions in coffee shops, playing basketball at the local court, joining a book club, going to a local playground with one's children, talking with strangers during an airplane ride, inviting people to church, and many other ways, Christians can evangelize the lost and work to bring people to saving faith, just as Edwards did in 1734. Pastor Mark Driscoll has written helpful material about this kind of life in books like *Radical Reformission*, which details how he sought to reach the lost people in Seattle in the early years of his ministry. For many of us, simply attempting to get to know lost people and becoming involved in our communities and neighborhoods would make a great first step.

Loving and Esteeming the Local Church

Christians need to remember that doctrine is not only to be defended, as Edwards did in his Yale address, but to be offered as a feast of faith, as Edwards did in his evangelistic preaching. In particular, the good news of salvation, including the idea of justification, need not be seen as a mere set of beliefs, but as a means to passionate trust in the Lord. Believers can practically act on such a conviction by esteeming the gospel-centered teaching and preaching of the local church. Taking the sermon seriously is a great way for a Christian to begin to actually enjoy doctrine. If one would approach the sermon and the Sunday service not as a spiritual doctor's appointment, a rote exercise, but as a feast of spiritual food, one would attain maturity and joy previously unthinkable for a less serious-minded Christian.

Each week, Edwards tried to lay out just such a meal for his people. He had eaten richly himself during the week as he prepared his message. If Christians would emulate Edwards's example, whether as a pastor or a layperson, they would acquire a great love for truth, much as one acquires a taste for fruits and vegetables after years of hot dogs and nachos. As Christians, we must train ourselves both to love rich teaching and to leave doctrinal junk food behind. For more on this sort of living, see Thabiti Anyabwile's recent book *What Is a Healthy Church Member?*.

Reaching Children

*E*dwards showed great humility in embracing Whitefield's revival messages as a means of converting his family. Sometimes parents become territorial about the spiritual training of their children. Parents need to approach the salvation of their children with modesty and realize that God can and will use many different factors in conversion. On matters of faith, there is no place for a man or a woman to be proud. This applies to child raising as much as it does to our own spiritual lives. If a theological giant like Edwards sought assistance from gifted Christians in the salvation of his children, so too should we avail ourselves of sound teaching from a wide variety of people as we point our children to the hope we have in Christ.

CHAPTER 6

The Unseen Underworld

In the spring and summer of 1741, Jonathan Edwards delivered the sermon that etched him into the history books for centuries to come. "Sinners in the Hands of an Angry God," as it became known, turned Northampton and the Connecticut River Valley upside down and sent a message of ultimate reality through the colonies that echoes to this day. Nearly three hundred years after Edwards first preached it, it remains the most famous American sermon, and perhaps the most famous sermon of all time.

It all began on a hot summer day in 1741 in little Enfield, Massachusetts (now Connecticut, about 31 miles south of Northampton), when Jonathan stepped into the pulpit and began expounding on Deuteronomy 32:35: "Their foot shall slide in due time." Though his tone was calm, his words were full of thunder. In sentence after dreadful sentence, Edwards laid out the torments that awaited unrepentant sinners in the afterlife, describing them with such force that one could almost see the fiery pit as the sermon unfolded. Beginning as he so often did with the relation of God to the sermon's subject, Edwards observed that God:

IS NOT ONLY ABLE TO CAST wicked men into hell, but he can most easily do it. Sometimes an earthly prince meets with a great deal of difficulty to subdue a rebel, that has found means to fortify himself, and has made himself strong by the numbers of his followers. But it is not so with God. There is no fortress that is any defense from the power of God. Though hand join in hand, and vast multitudes of God's enemies combine and associate themselves, they are easily broken in pieces: they are as great heaps of light chaff before the whirlwind; or large quantities of dry stubble before devouring flames. We find it easy to tread on and crush a worm that we see crawling on the earth; so 'tis easy for us to cut or singe a slender thread that anything hangs by; thus easy is it for God when he pleases to cast his enemies down to hell. What are we, that we should think to stand before him, at whose rebuke the earth trembles, and before whom the rocks are thrown down? (*Works* 22, 405)

Edwards had long sought to develop his writing style, to make it simultaneously pungent and precise, rich and enveloping. He wanted his words to communicate transcendent concepts and ideas. In "Sinners in the Hands of an Angry God," he demonstrated that he had found his voice.

As in "A Divine and Supernatural Light," Edwards's words in "Sinners" brought his hearers to another place. His language and logic were relentless. He turned his subject like a diamond just a few degrees with each description to catch the attention of his hearers. This was no mere intellectual exercise, however, no story telling time. Edwards preached to save the souls of his hearers. The earth opened up as Edwards mixed illustrations, doctrinal statements, and plain exhortation to illuminate the true nature of hell, the realm where flames devour and men's souls are continually anguished. An awful majesty loomed over this terrible scene, for God ruled over hell, Edwards declared, a figure of fury toward all who had rejected Him. Unlike the deity fixed in many minds, Edwards taught his hearers that God was no buddy in the sky, but a ferocious conqueror of all who had defied Him. If massive "rocks" were "thrown down" in God's presence, how could human sinners expect to stand before the holy Lord of heaven and earth?

The Power of Satan

Another figure loomed large in the supernatural world that Edwards depicted, a shadowy, sinister figure who desired to destroy everyone he could:

THE DEVIL STANDS READY to fall upon them and seize them as his own, at what moment God shall permit him. They belong to him; he has their souls in his possession, and under his dominion. The Scripture represents them as his "goods," Luke 11:21. The devils watch them; they are ever by them, at their right hand; they stand waiting for them, like greedy hungry lions that see their prey, and expect to have it, but are for the present kept back; if God should withdraw his hand, by which they are restrained, they would in one moment fly upon their poor souls. The old serpent is gaping for them; hell opens its mouth wide to receive them; and if God should permit it, they would be hastily swallowed up and lost. (*Works* 22, 406–7)

In Edwards's mind, the figure of Satan existed as a very real presence, a powerful force for evil. Commanding minions who obeyed his every whim, Satan stood ready to devour lost souls, "gaping for them." The scene is akin to a modern horror film of the darkest sort and accords with biblical accounts of Satan (see 1 Peter 5:8, for example). According to Peter and other biblical authors, Satan does not conduct his work of terror from a position of weakness. Though he is bounded by the will of God (see Job 1), Satan roams over all the earth, observing it, and roaring with bloodlust. He zeroes in on those who give themselves over to sin, feeding their hunger for evil until he secures their damnation. As they suffer his torments, he watches over them, gleeful, victorious, roaring with pride, hungry for more. His thirst for souls is never sated, and until Christ returns to earth and defeats him in the last battle, he will not cease to destroy men, women, and children from every corner of the world.

The Hopelessness of the Sinner

When Edwards preached "Sinner," the weight of this description and others caused many in the audience to weep and wail and even scream in terror. The preacher proclaimed that God and Satan stood close at hand to the unrepentant sinner, waiting for the right moment to unleash wrath and destruction on them. The wicked, Edwards declared in no uncertain terms, had no friend, no savior. The dark lion waited to pounce; the majestic sovereign stayed his hand for the moment, but would swing it like a hammer in due time. Having sketched these roles, Edwards then focused on the condition of the sinner, urging that:

> YOUR WICKEDNESS MAKES YOU as it were heavy as lead, and to tend downwards with great weight and pressure towards hell; and if God should let you go, you would immediately sink and swiftly descend and plunge into the bottomless gulf, and your healthy constitution, and your own care and prudence, and best contrivance, and all your righteousness, would have no more influence to uphold

you and keep you out of hell, than a spider's web would have to stop a falling rock. (*Works* 22, 410)

Edwards diagnosed the presumptuousness of the unredeemed human heart in words designed to scorch away its natural narcissism:

WERE IT NOT THAT so is the sovereign pleasure of God, the earth would not bear you one moment; for you are a burden to it; the creation groans with you; the creature is made subject to the bondage of your corruption, not willingly; the sun don't willingly shine upon you to give you light to serve sin and Satan; the earth don't willingly yield her increase to satisfy your lusts; nor is it willingly a stage for your wickedness to be acted upon; the air don't willingly serve you for breath to maintain the flame of life in your vitals, while you spend your life in the service of God's enemies. God's creatures are good, and were made for men to serve God with, and don't willingly subserve to any other purpose, and groan when they are abused to purposes so directly contrary to their nature and end. And the world would spew you out, were it not for the sovereign hand of him who hath subjected it in hope. (*Works* 22, 410)

The Northampton preacher recalibrated the presuppositions of his hearers. Many of them, he supposed, believed that God represented some sort of benevolent father who sought only to serve people and make them happy. The earth made by God and all that was in it, then, existed solely to please and gratify human beings. Man, fundamentally, was right, and knew what he deserved and should have. He had a natural right to grace and could justifiably curse God if such did not come to him. Against such a depraved mindset, Edwards offered a vision of God in which God was holy, sovereign, the possessor of self-determinacy, and the just recipient of worship and service. Edwards removed man from the place he naturally claimed, the throne of God, and restored God's proper rulership. His words exploded the presumption of the human heart by showing that human beings only lived and breathed at all because of the divine will, the "mere pleasure" as he later put it, of the Lord. Like gravity to a stone, the weight of God's justice drove sinners to the hell they deserved, with only God's goodness staying this irresistible force.

The Awesome Mercy of Christ

Having laid out in great detail the agonies of hell and the frailty of human existence, Edwards summoned his hearers to the mercy of Christ. His sermon had dashed their false hopes and exploded their arrogance. Now, the preacher exhorted "everyone that is yet out of Christ, and hanging over the pit of hell, whether they be old men and women, or middle aged, or young people, or little children, now hearken to the loud calls of God's Word and providence." Speaking with great urgency, Edwards stated that "God seems now to be hastily gathering in his elect in all parts of the land; and probably the bigger part of adult persons that ever shall be saved, will be brought in now in a little time," a pronouncement that captured the sense of drama and immediacy that the young pastor felt. With a final warning, Edwards called to his hearers to seize eternal life while they still could:

> THEREFORE LET EVERYONE that is out of Christ, now awake and fly from the wrath to come. The wrath of almighty God is now undoubtedly hanging over great part of this congregation: let everyone fly out of Sodom: "Haste and escape for your lives, look not behind you, escape to the mountain, lest you be consumed" [Gen. 19:17]. (*Works* 22, 418)

When Edwards ended the sermon, people cried out audibly for salvation. The master craftsman had made a deep impression on his hearers. He preached his message without relish or pomposity, and opened up the spiritual realm for all to see. Edwards's sermon captured the biblical reality that a vast battle between God and Satan rages for the souls of mankind. Many people responded to this new vision with repentance born of fear and gratefulness to the Savior, Jesus Christ, whose atoning death and resurrection made possible the forgiveness of sins, the satisfaction of God's wrath, and the attainment of eternal life in heaven with God. This, after all, was Edwards's aim: not to merely scare his people or share frightening stories, but to cause them to look honestly on their sin and their deserved fate, and then to joyfully flee to Christ, the sinner's substitute, for salvation.

Discerning Saving Faith

The good effects of Edwards's preaching continued throughout the summer as the pastor preached "Sinners in the Hands of an Angry God." He saw numerous people profess faith in the new birth and witnessed a spirit of reverence and awe spread in his congregation. Even with such observably positive results, however, a group of Protestant pastoral colleagues spoke against the revivals Edwards led, decrying them as mere "enthusiasm" that would pass in short order. Edwards took care to respond to the awakening's detractors, delivering an address at Yale's commencement in September 1741 entitled "Distinguishing Marks of a Work of the Spirit of God." In this nuanced yet vigorous defense of the revivals, Edwards laid out a theology of conversion, detailing the marks of a redeemed heart alongside "signs" that neither proved nor disproved the claim of conversion.

First, Edwards covered the neutral marks that could not conclusively provide evidence either a true or false work of God in His people. "A work is not to be judged of," wrote Edwards, "by any effects on the bodies of men; such as tears, trembling, groans, loud outcries, agonies of body, or the failing of bodily strength" (*Works* 4, 230). Positive signs included love for Christ, opposition to Satan, reverence for God's Word, and love for God and man. The address illuminated the Christian's experience of these signs. In reflecting on the way that the Holy Spirit produces love for God in the hearts of the truly converted, Edwards explained that the Spirit "works in them an admiring, delightful sense of the excellency of Jesus Christ, representing him as 'the chief among ten thousands, altogether lovely' [Song of Solomons 5:10, 16], and makes him precious to the soul" (*Works* 4, 256). The Spirit causes intense delight in the heart of the Christian as He "makes the attributes of God as revealed in the Gospel and manifested in Christ, delightful objects of contemplation; and makes the soul to long after God and Christ, after their presence and communion, and acquaintance with them, and conformity to them; and to live so as to please and honor them." This love flowed into the daily life of the Christian as the Spirit "quells contentions among men, and gives a spirit of peace and goodwill, excites to acts of outward kindness and earnest desires of the salvation of others' souls; and causes a delight in those that appear as the children of God and followers of Christ" (*Works* 4, 256).

"Distinguishing Marks" displays a pastoral theology of the richest sort. The text goes beyond a defense of the revivals and delves into far deeper matters involving the nature of Christianity. Edwards could write soaring treatises about philosophical matters or theological quandaries, but he was fundamentally a pastor who wanted to help his congregation figure out the Christian life.

Making Christianity Clear

Although his address at Yale began as an apology, it soon turned toward a biblical picture of the converted life. As with so much of the preacher's writings, theological description bled over into exhortative meditation. Edwards was not immune to a snarky exchange, as future years would make clear, but in his hands, even a self-defensive polemic against his detractors could become a contemplation of the glories of Christ and the beauty of living for Him through the Spirit. Edwards never sought simply to describe, but to awaken. The exercise of carefully studying the marks of rich Christian living naturally leads the heart to yearn for such character. In "Distinguishing Marks," one picks up the scent of fresh, vivid faith, a discovery that leads one to hunger for that which is described.

A Stormy Season of Ministry

The early-1740s brought considerable encouragement to Edwards as he observed positive results from his preaching and leadership of his church. The mid-1740s, however, proved challenging for the preacher, now recognized as the leader of the "New Lights," the enthusiastic promoters of evangelical revival. His congregation, seemingly transformed during Whitefield's visit and the subsequent preaching of Jonathan, grew lax in their faith and failed to respond passionately to much of Edwards's pulpit ministry. Edwards approached his work with deadly seriousness and interpreted this laxity as a personal responsibility. He responded by ramping up the rhetoric of his sermons, chastising his congregation over and over for their spiritual laziness.

In 1744, Edwards attempted to discipline a number of young men in his church who had gotten hold of a midwives' manual depicting matters of pregnancy and then acted in sexually suggestive ways to a number of young girls. The behavior was sinful by any standard, but Edwards approached it as a watershed moment for his flock, believing that he had to publicly condemn the act from the pulpit, doing so even as he sought to discipline the young men. The affair went badly, and the youths rebelled against their pastor. Edwards could not reconcile with them, which left a bad taste in many mouths.

Edwards picked this testy period to begin conversations about an increase in his pastoral salary. The process lasted for no less than three years and involved many publicly embarrassing moments for the pastor. Though an eminent minister and the product of a revered family, Edwards had to fight tooth and nail for his raise, and he had to promise after receiving the increase that he would not again raise the matter. Edwards did live at a high standard in comparison with his parishioners, but he also worked in an era in which pastors led their communities and occupied a loftier social position than today. Nonetheless, he showed an ill-tempered spirit at times and did not always make the process of negotiation an easy one.

Continued Defense of the Revivals

Circumstances improved when he published the *Treatise Concerning Religious Affections* in 1746. The text expanded on the work Edwards had done in his "Distinguishing Marks" address at Yale in 1741. The book incited some controversy, but has proven to be a classic work in the field of pastoral theology. It acted as a further affirmation by Edwards of the veracity of the Great Awakening and demonstrated his continued belief in the reality of conversion produced through evangelistic preaching. When visited by the Holy Spirit, the encounter of conscience and content created saving faith in Jesus Christ. Though some still denounced this method of sermonizing, Edwards defended it until his death. Preaching for him was not merely about forming strong character or delving deeply into a passage. Edwards aimed at transformation. For that, only the gospel would do.

Further Controversy

Controversy flared again in 1747 when Edwards publicly pressed a young man, Thomas Wait, to marry a girl, Martha Root, whom Wait had impregnated. One senses the tension of the ordeal in a brief, sparse letter from Edwards to a fellow minister involved in the council adjudicating the matter: "The number of the chosen council is but small," Edwards wrote in taut prose, "and if some should fail, the design might fail" (*Works* 16, 222). The design did fail. Wait refused to marry Root, bringing further embarrassment to Edwards and leaving him wondering about the extent of his pastoral influence. Edwards's attempts to model and to exert a holy example upon his church and town had at times succeeded, as seen in the revivals his preaching produced. At other times, however, his efforts failed, and he often felt personally responsible.

Like any Christian, the pastoral leader and literary luminary of colonial New England knew his trials, both personally inflicted and externally caused. Unfortunately, several more visited him before the contentious decade of the 1740s ended, including one that robbed him of two of his dearest friends in the world.

Applying Edwards's Life and Ideas

Beyond Mere Belief

*A*s a pastor, Jonathan tried to engage his people with the realities behind their spiritual beliefs. Many people held a cognitive belief in heaven and hell. But Edwards wanted this knowledge to blossom into a personal connection with the spiritual world. His preaching ushered his hearers into the unseen spiritual world where God and the devil battled for the souls of sinners. Jonathan was able to bring his people to a deeper personal understanding of spiritual things because he lived in this realm on a daily basis. He did not simply read his Bible in the morning and then go on to live his life as if God and Satan did not exist. He meditated often on the things he could not see and thus made them part of his worldview.

Christians today need to work to understand the deeper things of faith that our modern world helps us to easily forget. Though it seems strange to say in this age, we should think about hell. We should not direct our minds only to pleasant things and passing diversions. We need to take the spiritual world seriously, and to meditate on it and think about it in the course of our daily lives. Part of the reason why so many of us struggle to find assurance and depth in our faith is that we simply do not think much about heaven and hell and the God who rules over each.

Edwards was able to live with great seriousness and passion because he knew where he did not want to go and where he did not want other people to go. He studied hell and often remembered what God had saved him from. He did not simply think about where he was going after death; he thought about where, but for the grace of God, he would surely have gone. This contemplation fueled his passion for the Lord and drove him to live a serious and purposeful life. Because Edwards looked deeply into the reality of eternal torment, he was equipped to live a life of great spiritual intensity that pointed countless people away from hell and toward heaven.

One certainly doesn't need to be a pastor to exert this kind of influence on peers, friends, and family. Christians of all kinds can model interest in the afterlife. We need simply to take God, His Word, and heaven and hell seriously, and then to transfer that seriousness to a pattern of life that motivates people to consider unseen things that seem otherworldly but will soon become reality.

The Duty of Examination

*E*dwards's work to examine his life and his church members' lives for the marks of conversion sets a great example for Christians and churches today. On a regular basis, we should take stock of our spiritual lives. In our churches, we should emphasize the marks of conversion so that people know what it means to be a Christian. Edwards's writings on this subject are some of the best for understanding the redeemed life. Believers of all backgrounds can help fellow church members to find assurance and conviction by studying and talking about the biblical marks of conversion. Many people today waver in their faith because they have little understanding of the spiritual fruits. Studying this subject will lead both to conviction over patterns of sin and fresh assurance for believers that their contradictory behavior does not necessarily signal unbelief, but rather the need for fresh dependence upon the Spirit.

The Importance of Unity

*T*he difficulties Edwards had with his congregation remind us that we must all strive to preserve unity in the body. Even if we have a just claim to make, we should pick our battles wisely and avoid a spirit of presumption and contentiousness. Edwards was justified in making his salary request, but he might have chosen a better time and manner to present it. Part of Christian identity is bearing with others in grace; Paul instructed the Philippian Christians to humbly "count others more significant than yourselves" (Philippians 2:3). It will take wisdom and the Spirit's influence to work this out in the life of the church, but this process is essential and will save the body much division and pain. We should seek to emulate Edwards in his care for his family, but we should also pursue charity and humility wherever possible.

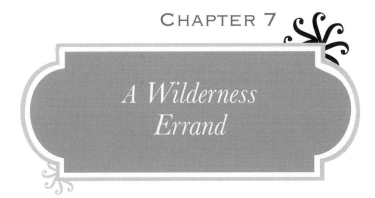

CHAPTER 7

A Wilderness Errand

The Story of David Brainerd

While Edwards loved each of his children and spent much time with them, Jerusha, the second child, shared her father's passionate faith and enjoyed a special closeness with him. Of all the Edwards offspring, Jerusha responded most to her father's teaching and even as a teenager showed a desire to offer a sacrificial witness to the lost around her.

It was not surprising that she got along particularly well with a young visitor to the Edwards household in 1747. David Brainerd, a Yale graduate and a missionary to the Indians in

Stockbridge, MA, came to the home after falling terribly ill during his missionary work. Brainerd had made Edwards's acquaintance while a student at Yale. A devout person, Brainerd impressed Edwards with his seriousness, though Edwards worried from their first meeting about the young man's lack of personal balance and melancholy disposition. He maintained contact with Brainerd during the missionary's time among the Indians of Stockbridge and served as a counselor to the gifted but often-depressed Brainerd.

Brainerd's ministry had started off rockily. He labored to communicate with the Indians whom he evangelized, had no English-speaking friends around him, and struggled to build adequate shelter and find sufficient food. Months passed, and the young Christian made little meaningful contact with the Indians. Yet he preached the gospel over and over, attempting to make clear the most basic matters of the Christian faith to a people who had little natural connection with the message. Brainerd repeatedly despaired and wrote in his diary of a desire to leave the work. When seemingly at his lowest point, however, light broke out. Multitudes of the Indian people expressed interest in the gospel. Soon, many professed belief in it to their family members and became observably faithful to the Bible. The change was astounding. Brainerd's heart soared. After a long season of struggle, the Lord had smiled on his work, and drawn dozens of lost people to Himself.

Brainerd's Illness

In the process of ministering to the Indians of Stock-bridge, Brainerd had often abused his body by sleeping and eating little in order to evangelize. The results proved disastrous, and in the fall of 1746 Brainerd set out from Stock-bridge to rest at the home of family. He did not complete the journey, but collapsed in the home of a friend and sponsor, Jonathan Dickinson, and remained there for several months. After his time there, Brainerd moved from home to home, never fully recovering, until he landed at the Edwards's home in May 1747.

Brainerd's health improved under the excellent care of Sarah Edwards and others. The Edwards home was always open to needy people with whom the Edwards had acquaintance, and Jonathan personally gave large sums of money to needy people in his church and town. He had a burden to help others, though he rarely, if ever, mentioned such deeds. He and Brainerd enjoyed much conversation and fellowship together. He loved to hear Brainerd pray, for the young man exhibited fervent piety and sound theology.

Mentoring the Future Generation

Edwards clearly saw Brainerd as one to mentor. Edwards mentored a large number of young men in his pastoral career, informally training a corps of theologically minded pastors and Christian leaders from his home in Northampton. Though his house was already filled with numerous inhabitants, including children and slaves, Edwards made training the next generation of pastors a priority and invited future pastors and theologians to stay with him and use his impressive library for a season of study and learning. The mind boggles to know how Jonathan accomplished this goal in the midst of family life, church oversight, and writing, but he did. At meals, in snatches of conversation while working in his study, while riding for exercise, Jonathan kindly reached out to a good number of young men and imparted wisdom and a vision of ministry to them. The Lord honored these efforts. Years after Jonathan's death, numerous churches across New England benefited from skilled pastor-theologians who trained under the Northampton pastor.

The Shamefulness of Slavery

It should be noted that Edwards was able to accomplish as much as he did in part because he bought into the viability of slavery. This is a massive stain on the reputation of a great Christian man. Though Edwards did treat his slaves well, and though he believed in and taught about the spiritual equality of all people before the Lord, he failed to adequately apply spiritual truth to his everyday life. Even so faithful a Christian and so biblically concerned a believer as Edwards had his blind spots—some of them, like slavery, shameful in great measure. Those of us who celebrate his legacy must square with this offensive aspect of his life even as we remember others of more positive character.

Brainerd and Jerusha

Brainerd and Edwards enjoyed a happy season of mutual enrichment until Brainerd set off for Boston in the summer to improve his health through horseback riding. Brainerd did not travel alone. Jerusha Edwards rode with the young missionary, keeping him company and watching over his health. The two likely talked for hours, enjoying conversation about spiritual things, gazing at the countryside, enjoying companionship with a like-minded person. As they traveled, David's condition worsened. Once in Boston, Brainerd abruptly neared the edge of mortality. He suffered from tuberculosis, and his doctors informed him that he could die at any moment. He rested for weeks in the city, with Jerusha constantly by his side.

In late July, Brainerd had recovered enough strength to return to Northampton. Not even thirty years of age, he possessed the body of a much older man, and had to travel slowly to Edwards's home. Once the party reached their destination, Brainerd sank into bed, rarely rising through the late summer and early fall. He edited the diary he had written as a missionary, talked at length with Jerusha, and spent time with Jonathan, his mentor. Though this was a happy season, Brainerd's hour drew near.

In early October, David and his friends knew that death was not far away. Over the next few days, the missionary said his goodbyes. His words to Jerusha were poignant: "Dear Jerusha, are you willing to part with me? I am quite willing to part with you: I am willing to part with all my friends: I am willing to part with my dear brother John; although I love him the best of any creature living: I have committed him and all my friends to God, and can leave them with God" (Marsden, 326). The statement testified to Brainerd's profoundly spiritual orientation. He lived with the realities of the spiritual world on his mind. As with Edwards, God was close at hand for Brainerd.

Brainerd's next word to Jerusha showed deep affection for his spiritual companion. "[I]f I thought I should not see you and be happy with you in another world, I could not bear to part with you. But we shall spend an happy eternity together!" (Marsden, 326). Two days later, on October 9, 1747, he breathed his last, leaving Jerusha, Jonathan, and the Edwards family heartbroken.

Jerusha's Death

Several months later the family continued to recover from Brainerd's passing. In February 1748, Jerusha also fell deeply ill. After a week of suffering, the young woman died in the arms of her family. Edwards was grief-stricken. Jerusha was "generally esteemed the flower of the family," as the pastor told a friend (Marsden, 325), and the family felt a "melancholy absence" after losing her (*Works* 16, 245). Edwards memorialized his daughter in a moving sermon. Jerusha had been "remarkably weaned" from the world and frequently "declared in words, showed in deeds" that she was "ever more ready to deny herself, earnestly inquiring in every affair which way should most glorify God" (Marsden, 328). Jerusha's death and conflicts with his congregation cast a shadow over most of the 1740s, and Jonathan struggled at times to stoke his heart. The sweet things of life could become the saddest. This reality yielded another irony, however: it was often in these hardest of hard times that the kindness of the Lord became most apparent.

The Legacy of David Brainerd

Edwards memorialized his spiritual son, Brainerd, in *An Account of the Life of the Late Reverend Mr. David Brainerd*, published in 1749 after Edwards finished a biographical essay on Brainerd and the editing of the missionary's journals. He published the text for the ages, hoping it would stir up Christians of present and future generations to embrace missionary work. Brainerd's diary captured the marrow of difficult evangelistic labor even as it presented the reader with a challenging portrait of a life consecrated to the Lord.

Brainerd exhibited, Edwards wrote, "such an illustrious pattern of humility, divine love, discreet zeal, self-denial, obedience, patience, resignation, fortitude, meekness, forgiveness, compassion, benevolence, and universal holiness, as neither men nor angels ever saw before." This man "was a minister of the Gospel, and one who was called to unusual services in that work, whose ministry was attended with very remarkable and unusual events," for he "was the instrument of a most remarkable awakening" (*Works* 7, 90). Edwards's effort to honor Brainerd and perpetuate his legacy paid off in abundance. Modern missionary experts credit *The Life of David Brainerd* with sparking the modern missions movement, which has led to the sending of thousands upon thousands of missionaries to every corner of the globe.

A Trying Hour

Edwards's time with Brainerd lifted his spirits for a period as the two enjoyed deep friendship. When Brainerd and Jerusha passed away, however, Edwards grieved for an extended period. His difficulties, however, would not pass for some time. In a shocking turn of events, Jonathan Edwards's congregation fired him in 1750. The magnitude of this event requires some brief background explanation.

Edwards's grandfather, Solomon Stoddard, had instituted a controversial policy in the Northampton church during his tenure as pastor. Observing his society shift away from interest in Christianity, but wanting people to remain connected to the church, Stoddard came to believe that he should offer the Lord's Supper to all who attended the service regardless of whether they professed and demonstrated faith in Christ as Savior. This decision placed Stoddard in disagreement with many evangelical ministers, who had followed historical trends in allowing only believers to take of the bread and the cup per certain passages of 1 Corinthians 10 and 11 (see especially 10:16–17). Stoddard, however, saw the Lord's Supper as a means of evangelism. In participating in the holy rite, he argued, people would come face to face with the reality of Christian faith. They might well respond by receiving Christ as their savior for the first time.

Jonathan had long disagreed with his venerated grandfather, yet he did not want to ruffle feathers unnecessarily. He sought to step carefully in changing the policy of the church on admission to the supper. He waited for over two decades before introducing the matter to his congregation, at which point he argued forcefully for his view that only believers ought to take communion. Jonathan believed that allowing unbelievers to partake of the elements invited the Lord's judgment upon them and the minister who served them. He had published his view the year before in 1749 in a careful but characteristically forceful manuscript entitled *An Humble Inquiry in the rules of the Word of God, Concerning the Qualification Requisite to a Compleat Standing and Full Communion in the Visible Christian Church.* Edwards thought at the time that the church would follow his lead and change their doctrinal position on the matter. As he wrote to a friend, "I am not sure but that my people, in length of time and with great difficulty, might be brought to yield the point as to the qualifications for the Lord's Supper, though that is very uncertain" (*Works* 16, 283).

Edwards's Ejection

Whether naïve or just optimistic, Edwards's hopes were soon dashed when his handling of a difficult matter raised a storm in the church. Edwards refused to admit a young man without testimony of salvation to membership, causing many to oppose him. The church and Edwards engaged in a protracted public struggle over the matter, with both sides expressing frustration. Edwards was not permitted to hold a conversation with his congregation that would have allowed him to clarify his decision regarding the young man's membership. Bad turned to worse, and on June 22, 1750, the greatest preacher America has ever known was ejected from his church.

Edwards and his family were stunned. Though Edwards did not shy away from strong leadership that led at times to controversy, the family did not expect so late in life to lose their ministry and all that came with it—their home, their reputation, and their future in Northampton. Jonathan enjoyed a tremendous reputation among colonial pastors. His firing caused him great embarrassment and wrenched him from an established pattern of writing, preaching, and leading that he had carried out for decades. Yet Edwards believed strongly in the providence of God, and he trusted the Lord to lead him through this trial. In his last sermon as the pastor of the Northampton church, he concluded his tenure with a word full of pathos to the people he had so long shepherded:

HAVING BRIEFLY MENTIONED these important articles of advice, nothing remains; but that I now take my leave of you, and bid you all farewell; wishing and praying for your best prosperity. I would now commend your immortal souls to him, who formerly committed them to me; expecting the day, when I must meet you again before him, who is the Judge of quick and dead. I desire that I may never forget this people, who have been so long my special charge, and that I may never cease fervently to pray for your prosperity. May God bless you with a faithful pastor, one that is well acquainted with his mind and will, thoroughly warning sinners, wisely and skillfully searching professors, and conducting you in the way to eternal blessedness. May you have truly a burning and shining light set up in this candlestick; and may you, not only for a season, but during his whole life, and that a long life, be willing to rejoice in his light.

The sermon closed with this:

AND LET US ALL REMEMBER, and never forget our future solemn meeting, on that great day of the Lord; the day of infallible decision, and of the everlasting and unalterable sentence, Amen. (Kimnach, 240–1)

Pastoring to the end, Jonathan Edwards concluded his career in Northampton.

Finding a New Work

At age forty-six, Edwards found himself out of work. The irony of this situation would have been rich if it were not so bitter. This was a tough time for Edwards. Though the previous fifteen years had brought considerable hardship and challenge to him, he continually rededicated himself to serving the Lord. Talented and focused as he was, Edwards could not avoid suffering. He could, however, face suffering from a confident belief in God's goodness and power that enabled him to fight his way to joy in a fallen world.

Edwards's situation weighed on his mind, however, for he had a large family to feed. He filled the Northampton pulpit, ironically, but could not do so indefinitely. He also preached in other locations, including Boston, Middletown, CT, and Longmeadow, MA. In February 1751, though, Edwards found his next calling: he took over the Stockbridge Indian Mission in Massachusetts. Edwards had long supported missionary causes, and he had helped to fund this mission, sending Brainerd to evangelize in the area. The little village of Stockbridge had raised enough funds to build a church and several schools. The missionary efforts in the town had gone well, with over 175 Mahican and Mohawk Indians being baptized. Edwards and his family hoped to continue the good work and moved into town, side-by-side with the Indians whom they sought to evangelize. The new work had begun.

Reclaiming Stockbridge

Fifty miles west of Northampton on the Massachusetts border, Stockbridge was a frontier town, small but full of factions, including one containing members of Edwards's extended family, the Williamses. The Williamses were small-town elites who ran things and made life difficult when they could not do so. They initially made life very challenging for Jonathan as they ran schools for Indian children but with little concern for the physical and spiritual welfare of the students and their families. Edwards was not immune to certain racist attitudes and actions (as noted, he held slaves over the course of his adult life), but he also showed clear concern for people whom others neglected. Over a period of months, Edwards bravely fought the Williamses, ultimately winning control of the school. He did so not to win power for its own sake, but to help the Indians, to educate them so that they could learn the faith and participate in colonial society.

In this incident one sees some of Edwards's strongest virtues: Courage, conviction, devotion to the spiritual good of others, and a willingness to persevere in a just cause. Jonathan brought great blessing to the Indians and the town of Stockbridge by his courage. He stood up to the ill-minded power brokers of the town and watched as the Lord honored his efforts by granting him victory in the feud.

A Contextualized Ministry

The controversy took much of Edwards's time and energy and shows how sin and selfishness can end up consuming large amounts of time for Christians. The missionary, though, did not lose sight of his primary calling. Jonathan devoted himself to reaching the Indians. He contextualized his message for them, preaching expository messages in stark, simple language that made the fundamental claims of Christianity abundantly clear. Compare the following excerpt from a sermon on 2 Peter 1:19 to Edwards's previous preaching in Northampton:

> YOU SEE HOW IT IS [in] the spring. When the sun shines on the earth and trees, it gives 'em new life, makes the earth look green. It causes flowers to appear and give a good smell.
>
> So it is in the heart of a man when the light of God's Word shines into it. Wisdom and knowledge in religion is better than silver or gold and all the riches of the world.
>
> The light, when it shines into the heart, is sweeter than the honey, and the gospel will be a pleasant to you when you come to understand it. (Sermons, 110)

Edwards wisely tailored his message to his audience. He knew that if he tried to preach in the same high-flown style that he deployed in Northampton, his message would fly straight over the heads of his hearers. Thus, he contextualized his preaching, using simple phrases, relevant analogies, and direct language. The above sermon is set against the backdrop of nature, the world in which the Indians lived and easily understood. Edwards was not merely a master wordsmith, but a wise evangelist, employing all of his abilities to reach the particular people under his watch.

The Dawn of a New Season

The Edwards family had successfully resettled. Under Edwards's leadership, the family adapted nicely to life on the frontier. Times were sometimes tough, and life was certainly harder than it had been in Northampton, but Jonathan and Sarah continued to nurture their large family and to lead them well spiritually. Even under the constant threat of attack from hostile Indians, the family prospered. When reports of approaching warriors reached the town, Edwards and Sarah took what measures they could and trusted the Lord with the results. Such scares occurred frequently in the settlement. It was not safe, to be sure, but it was home. In one sense, Stockbridge is a fitting metaphor for all of Edwards's life—and beyond this, for the life of all Christians in a world in which believers must necessarily be strangers in a strange land.

Applying Edwards's Life and Ideas

Mentoring the Next Generation

*T*he way in which Edwards mentored a young and dying David Brainerd presents an excellent model for contemporary Christians. Whether we target missionaries or young moms, construction workers or professional athletes, all Christians can mentor someone and lead them to spiritual maturity. Jonathan trained a large group of pastors and theologians over the years. Though our target group may differ, we will find abundant blessings if we simply make the time to train young Christians in the faith. Our mentoring need not be fancy or creative; we could simply read a helpful theological book together and discuss it. In the course of doing so, we can share the wisdom we've gained in our own Christian walk. The effects of such engagement are difficult to quantify, but investment in even one person's life can make a tremendous spiritual difference. Indeed, it would be wonderful if entire churches caught the mentoring vision and created a culture of discipleship. This would contribute to unity and maturity on a previously unseen scale.

The Necessity of Self-Examination

*T*he fact that Edwards had slaves testifies that he was a man of his day who shared at least one of the massive sins of his era. If his sin resulted from a cultural blind spot, it is no less terrible. This sobering example reminds us to examine carefully the culture in which we live. Many Christians can tick off the ways in which their behavior differs from that of the world. But on a deeper, more fundamental level, are there whole areas of our lives that conform to the wicked patterns of the world? Are there blinders over our own eyes? Have we fallen prey to our materialistic culture such that we live carelessly, unaware of the suffering of many in our area and the church throughout the world? Are there ways in which we could, like Jonathan, care in a Christlike way for the poor and needy in our neighborhoods and in the church at home and abroad? We must constantly ask ourselves such questions. Furthermore, we need to listen to those who critique us and our denominations, our churches, and our families. They may be wrong in their critique of us on many points, but they may also be right on certain matters.

Persevering through Grief

*J*onathan's loss of his daughter and his reaction to it reminds us that we must ground ourselves in the Bible and in a rich relationship with our God. We must grow deep spiritual roots so that when trials come, we can withstand them and even glorify God in the midst of them. Jonathan's loss of his beloved daughter teaches us that we may be asked to give up what we most love in this life. This is a wrenching thought, but a reality we may have to face. None of us are immune to tragedy and despair. How important then that, like Edwards, we ground ourselves in the thick and fertile soil of God's Word. If we would endure all seasons of suffering, we must prepare accordingly, just as the Northampton pastor did.

Loving God's Shepherds

*T*he fact that America's greatest theologian was fired from his church is a source of historical shame. Edwards did not always make the right decision, and he was not free from sin, but his firing was a travesty. This sad event reminds Christians of all backgrounds to love their God-given pastors. We ought not to deify our pastors, but neither should we treat them as hired help. We should pay them well, treat them graciously, serve under them patiently, and generally seek to bless them by a godly congregational demeanor. We should not presume upon their time or think that their calendar belongs to us. Instead, we should treat our pastors with great care and respect, recognizing that the way that we care for them in some way reflects the very way we approach the One who is the Shepherd of us all.

Making the Most of Difficulties

*T*he way in which Edwards responded to his firing is a model for all Christians who find themselves in grievous circumstances. Terrible things can happen to faithful Christians, including the loss of a job, the onset of a disease, and difficult family situations. In such circumstances, we should embrace Edwards's model, and make the best of our situation. In his case, Jonathan used his firing as an opportunity to evangelize an unreached people and write important theological texts. All this after the most embarrassing moment of his life! If Edwards can make the most of his awkward situation, so can we. When we find ourselves in such moments, then, we must rededicate ourselves to prayer and to the will of God and seek a place of service to the Lord. It may be that, like Edwards, the Lord desires us to do significant work for His kingdom that we would not otherwise have discovered on our prior path. How important it is not to consider only our difficulties, but to consider the will of God that is moving through our difficulties and that ultimately will bring good to us and glory to Him (Romans 8:28; 31–39).

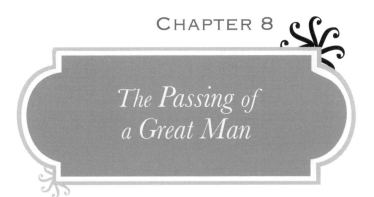

CHAPTER 8

The Passing of a Great Man

The Freedom of the Will

Stockbridge seemed to many to represent a dead-end for Edwards's ministerial career. Ironically, the relative quiet of the New England frontier allowed the pastor to carve out several master-works. From 1751 to 1757, Edwards wrote a series of texts that established him as America's greatest theologian. The first of these was *The Freedom of the Will*, a response to some theologians who argued that those who emphasized the sovereignty of God in salvation construed God as a puppet-master and humanity as a race of automatons. This group essentially believed that any attempt to preserve

God's power in the sphere of salvation resulted in the loss of human freedom. Not surprisingly, Edwards disagreed.

Edwards believed in the sovereignty of God over all things, including salvation. His conviction came from a careful reading of texts like Romans 9 and Ephesians 1. Yet, at the same time, Edwards believed that underneath the sovereignty of God, humanity possessed considerable agency that cooperated with the divine will to accomplish the purposes of God. Against robotic control of humans on one hand, and absolute freedom that rendered God a weak deity on the other, Edwards struck a balance between the two extremes with his position, commonly called *compatibilism*. This view, Edwards argued, adhered to the biblical picture of the divine and human wills in events like the exodus of Israel from Egypt (see Exodus 7–15). The human will acted freely in choosing its course in life, just as Pharaoh hardened his heart and chose not to release the Israelites on several occasions (see Exodus 9:34, for example). Though God was ultimately sovereign over all things, yet He worked out His sovereignty in such a way that humans did not live as robots but made real choices as free agents in the world.

In 1754, Edwards published these views in his book *Freedom of the Will*. The text represented the fruit of years of thinking on the matter. In page after page, the pastor-theologian relentlessly refuted the logic of his opponents and presented numerous scriptural passages supporting his view. In one section, Edwards wrote:

AND IF THAT FIRST ACT of the will, which determines and fixes the subsequent acts, be not free, none of the following acts, which are determined by it, can be free. If we suppose there are five acts in the train, the fifth and last determined by the fourth, and the fourth by the third, the third by the second, and the second by the first; if the first is not determined by the will, and so not free, then none of them are truly determined by the will: that is, that each of them are as they are, and not otherwise, is not first owing to the will, but to the determination of the first in the series, which is not dependent on the will, and is that which the will has no hand in the determination of.

And this being that which decides what the rest shall be, and determines their existence; therefore the first determination of their existence is not from the will. The case is just the same, if instead of a chain of five acts of the will, we should suppose a succession of ten, or an hundred, or ten thousand. If the first act be not free, being determined by something out of the will, and this determines the next to be agreeable to itself, and that the next, and so on; they are none of them free, but all originally depend on, and are determined by some cause out of the will: and so all freedom in the case is excluded, and no act of the will can be free, according to this notion of freedom. (*Works* 1, 173–4)

The passage—and the book more generally—is intellectually weighty. Many readers have grappled with it. The essential idea here and in the bulk of the text is this: freedom of the will, rightly defined, means that we can do whatever we want to do. All of our actions, then, proceed directly from our wills.

Those who opposed Edwards's position argued that he had bound the sinner's will such that the sinner could not choose what he desired (namely, God) but instead chose what he did not desire (unrighteousness). Edwards thought this response quite wrong. The key problem with a sinner, Edwards argued, is that though the human will is free, the sinful heart is corrupt, and thus leads mankind to naturally choose sin over righteousness. This act of choosing is free, because the will freely chooses, but the human heart is still bound with the chains of sin and thus can only choose God when the Holy Spirit regenerates the heart and causes it to know and love God.

Original Sin

Freedom of the Will sold well and continues to exert theological influence to this day, as do other of Edwards's later works. *Original Sin* (pub. 1758), written in this era and published after Edwards's death, offered a bracing apologetic for the traditional Puritan view of the natural human condition as inherently "depraved," or sinful. Some in Edwards's day argued instead that the human will was inherently good. Against this position and its adherents, Edwards contended that all humans demonstrated, from birth, a "tendency" to sin, regardless of whether this tendency manifested itself in public or private sins. No one had to be taught to sin, but everyone sinned naturally and continually. "A propensity to that sin which brings God's eternal wrath and curse (which has been proved to belong to the nature of man) is evil," Edwards wrote:

> NOT ONLY AS IT IS calamitous and sorrowful, ending in great natural evil; but it is odious too, and detestable; as, by the supposition, it tends to that moral evil, by which the subject becomes odious in the sight of God, and liable, as such, to be condemned, and utterly rejected and cursed by him.
>
> This also makes it evident, that the state which it has been proved mankind are in, is a corrupt state in a moral sense, that it is inconsistent with the fulfillment of the law of God, which is the rule of moral rectitude and goodness. That tendency, which is opposite to that which the moral law requires and insists upon, and prone to that which the moral law utterly forbids, and eternally condemns the subject for, is doubtless a corrupt tendency, in a moral sense. (*Works* 3, 129)

Here Edwards made the case that sin was not evil only because it created harmful conditions. Sin offended a holy God. All humans sinned and transgressed God's "rule of moral rectitude and goodness." The argument is simple, but devastating. If human nature is inherently good, why do all people display a "corrupt tendency"? Where else does the tendency for sin come from but the fall of Adam and Eve, the original sin? Through this act all became sinners, as Edwards read Romans 3 to argue. Whether one judged the matter by plain observation or biblical testimony, Edwards claimed, one could not avoid the reality of original sin in the hearts of mankind. Though many continue to disagree with Edwards's central contention, *Original Sin* is still referenced in the current day as a sure-footed guide to questions about fallen human nature and personal suffering in the world.

Life's Purpose and Virtue's Identity

The two other important books that Edwards completed while in Stockbridge were his *Dissertation Concerning the End for Which God Created the World* (pub. 1765) and *The Nature of True Virtue* (pub. 1765). The first tackled the heady question debated in countless dorm rooms: why does the world exist? Edwards provided a God-centric answer to the question in a voluminous text:

IN THE CREATURE'S KNOWING, esteeming, loving, rejoicing in, and praising God, the glory of God is both exhibited and acknowledged; his fullness is received and returned. Here is both an *emanation* and *remanation*. The refulgence shines upon and into the creature, and is reflected back to

> the luminary. The beams of glory come from God, and are
> something of God, and are refunded back again to their
> original. So that the whole is *of* God, and *to* God; and God
> is the beginning, middle and end in this affair. (*Works* 8, 531)

According to Edwards's theological calculations, all that exists
does so for the glory of God. Human beings carry the unique
ability to not merely please God through their existence, but
to do so through conscious joy in their Creator. Whenever
people seek to live according to the Scripture for the purpose
of glorifying the Lord, they effectively send back—or "remanate"—the original "emanations" of God's goodness. To live
for God, then, is to be a mirror and a conscious actor in the
drama of divine magnification. Edwards's view invested even
the most mundane existence with cosmic significance. All
who lived could participate in this work of "remanation" and
enter into the great story of God's creation. God and man
could draw near to one another and share the great work of
magnifying the glory of the Lord. This was not merely a theological proposition, but a narrative for life.

Edwards defined virtue, a hot topic in his day, along these
lines in the companion to *Dissertation*, a book entitled *The
Nature of True Virtue*. Over against some who defined virtue
in secular terms, believing it to be a matter of choosing good
over lesser options, Edwards framed the matter with characteristically God-centered dimensions. True virtue "most essentially consists in benevolence to Being in general." This
"Being" was God, though in Edwards's system the term

referred also to all of God's glorious creation. This virtue proceeded from an unselfish disposition that Edwards called "disinterested benevolence." Instead of seeking one's own glory, the virtuous person "being as it were under the sovereign dominion of *love to God*, does above all things seek the *glory of God*, and makes *this* his supreme, governing, and ultimate end" (*Works* 8, 559). The one who sought the glory of God would naturally be a virtuous, others-centered person. Though many people could perform isolated acts of benevolence, only the one focused on honoring God could perform the sweetest act the world could know: living kindly and sacrificially in service to the One who had Himself given His people all things. The chief gift, of course, was the Son of God, Jesus Christ, whose self-giving nature overturned the curse of death and sent a shock of glory throughout the universe that will ripple into eternity.

An Untouched Literary Legacy

Edwards had crafted these works throughout his time in Northampton and Stockbridge. He had written them in his mind and transferred portions to paper when he could. Though he did not live to see the positive impact of these important texts, he managed to finish a body of literature unlike any other ever produced by a pastor. It may well be that the world will never know another figure like Edwards, who stands alone in American church history as a writer and thinker.

Ironically, the posthumous publication of Edwards's most significant writings testifies eloquently to the concept of "disinterested benevolence." Seeking to redeem every moment for the glory of God, Edwards failed to publish most of these important treatises before his death. He thus failed to taste any significant reward for his efforts. This was not Edwards's purpose, of course. He sought simply to glorify his God with his mind and share his insights with God's people. As Edwards taught his readers, the Lord's gifts to his saints are not ends in themselves, but are "streams of glory" to be reflected back to heaven through the conscious attention of one's mind and heart. If one truly wished to follow Edwards's teaching, one would not ultimately praise the man or his talents. One would thank the Lord.

A Fresh Challenge

The work at Stockbridge proceeded without major interruption until 1757, when the Edwards family received yet another shock. The trustees of the College of New Jersey, a fledgling Christian institution, sought Jonathan for the school's presidency, a post vacated by the death of Edwards's son-in-law, Aaron Burr, father of the famous dueler. Edwards was initially inclined to reject the offer, but as he conferred with friends and trusted colleagues, his mind began to change. After a formal council of advisors encouraged him to take the post, Edwards accepted, though not without some resignation.

As noted previously, Stockbridge had afforded Edwards many opportunities to produce important texts, a situation the theologian was loath to give up. He had more books in the pipeline, including a project that covered the history of redemption and would likely have emerged as one of the most important books in Christian history. Though a college presidency appealed to many of Edwards's instincts, he also struggled to give up his missionary work. In addition, Edwards did not want to initiate the laborious and extended process of relocation so late in life with so large a family. He consented to the offer, however, writing a friend to request prayer in a tone that expressed a mixture of trepidation and humility. "I desire, Sir," he wrote to Gideon Hawley of Stockbridge, "your fervent prayer to God that I may have his favor and assistance in this great and arduous [task], for which I am so insufficient of myself" (*Works* 16, 738).

On February 16, 1758, the College of New Jersey, later Princeton University, installed Edwards as its president. He settled into the presidency in his first few weeks, working from the expansive president's home next to Nassau Hall, the college's academic building. He made initial contact with his students when he met with a group who wished to ask him theological questions. The meeting went nicely, as the students warmed to Edwards's capacious intellect and personal concern. The presidency was off to a good start. Edwards lived alone in this month, as he had traveled to Princeton without his family so that they could prepare for the process of moving.

The End of a Life

A week after he became president of the college, Edwards underwent an inoculation for smallpox, a dreaded disease in his day. Inoculations caused some controversy in the 1750s. They were a risky venture, but some physicians, including the Philadelphia doctor William Shippen, had proven their ability to safely treat patients. After receiving much counsel on the matter, Edwards decided to take the inoculation. Soon after the procedure, however, he found himself unable to swallow liquids. The disease consumed his body over a period of agonizing weeks while he battled starvation and fever with all the strength his thin frame could muster.

As the sun rose on March 22, 1758, Edwards knew that he would soon die. He called his daughter Lucy to his side and offered his final words. "Dear Lucy," he said in halting tones:

> IT SEEMS TO ME to be the will of God that I must shortly leave you; therefore give my kindest love to my dear wife, and tell her, that the uncommon union, which has so long subsisted between us, has been of such a nature, as I trust is spiritual, and therefore will continue forever; and I hope she will be supported under so great a trial, and submit cheerfully to the will of God. (Marsden, 494)

Before requesting a plain funeral, the loving father of ten addressed his children:

AND AS TO MY CHILDREN, you are now like to be left fatherless, which hope will be an inducement to you all to seek a Father, who will never fail you. (Marsden, 494)

Soon after, Edwards's breathing slowed, his heart stopped, and the pastor walked into his everlasting rest.

The End of an Uncommon Union

Sarah received the news a few days later while ill herself. Exhausted and stricken with grief, she found strength to write a few lines to her daughter Esther. Her words offer testimony to her confidence in God, even in the presence of almost unbearable grief:

A HOLY AND GOOD GOD has covered us with a dark cloud. Oh that we may kiss the rod [of reproof], and lay our hands on our mouths! The Lord has done it. He has made me adore his goodness, that we had him so long. But my God lives; and he has my heart. Of what a legacy my husband, and your father, has left us! We are all given to God: and there I am, and love to be. (Marsden, 495)

Without Jonathan, her rock and her love, Sarah struggled bravely to lead her family, but the task was too much. She fought illness and sleeplessness into the fall, when she contracted dysentery. On October 2, 1758, she passed away, joining her husband in heaven.

Having lost both of their parents, the Edwards's children soldiered on. Trained by godly parents, they went on to live fruitful Christian lives as homemakers, mothers, statesmen, theologians, and politicians. Succeeding generations of the family produced more of the same, leaving a familial legacy that is to the present day untouched by any other American family. The Lord honored his faithful servant by blessing Jonathan's family for generations to come.

The Legacy of Jonathan Edwards

The life of Jonathan Edwards was a monumental one. It was a life lived for the glory of God. Though a pastor, theologian, and a college president, Jonathan Edwards was fundamentally a follower of the Lord Jesus Christ. He accomplished much in his life, much that this text has celebrated, but all that he did began and ended with his sincere devotion to the Lord. Wherever he was, in whatever situation he found himself, whether a studious schoolboy or a towering intellectual, a chastened ex-pastor or an esteemed college president, Jonathan tenaciously pursued the Lord. He did so because he believed that he could only find lasting joy, taste true beauty, and know real forgiveness by worshipping the majestic God of the Bible. His life, like his faith, was dramatic, for Jonathan realized more than most that he did not live in a small and insignificant little world, but in a realm between heaven and hell where one served either God or Satan. Through dogged study of the Bible and regular meditation upon its realities, Edwards entered into the great battle for souls on the side of the Lord. He knew great trial in his life, and he struggled with sin all of his days, but he never stopped seeking the reward set before the saints of God.

Edwards's life is a living example to all the children of God in the current day, to put aside the things that hinder our faith and distract our focus. Though we may not serve as pastors, every believer can serve the local church devoted to Jesus Christ with all of their heart in whatever role God gifts them for. Though we may not possess a prodigious intellect, we can use our minds to study the Word and apply it to all of life. Though we may not articulate the faith with fresh insight and stirring language, we share the gospel and lead souls to Christ. It is not genius that the Lord seeks after, but faith. This Jonathan had; this we must have as well, in order that like him, we may one day meet the sovereign Lord of all the earth and bow before him in worship that will never cease.

Applying Edwards's Life and Ideas

Living Life for God's Glory

*E*arly on, Jonathan Edwards discovered the meaning of life—to joyfully glorify God. In fulfilling this end, Christians should take stock of their gifts. What natural strengths and abilities do we have? Once we have studied the Word, prayed about this question, and sought responses from our pastors and fellow church members, we should then ask, Where can I use these gifts for God's glory? What can I do with the life I have to "remanate," or reflect, glory back to God? What can I do to proclaim the gospel in this world? How can I advance God's kingdom? Who can I reach? These and similar questions, asked in concert with Bible study and wise counsel, will lead us to use our lives well.

Dying Well

*A*s we seek to live well, so should we seek to die well. Like Edwards, we must seize our season of death as a last opportunity to glorify our Lord. In our final act, we must hold fast to our faith and testify to those around us that we do not prepare for our termination, but our release.

Though we do not know when the last hour will come,

yet we can constantly prepare for it, just as Jonathan did. In fact, if we do so, we will find that living well and dying well are really the same thing for a Christian. To live well *is* to prepare to die and to stand before our Savior with a clear conscience. Without morbidity, but with a continual sense of confidence in the Lord and His plan, let us live with every ounce of strength, every atom of our being, for the glory of God. Let us follow in the steps of Jonathan Edwards, faithful witness, devout Christian, lover of God.

*A Life
Lived for God*

There is much to celebrate about the life of Jonathan Edwards. As we have seen in our brief survey of his life and thought, Edwards wore many hats in his day. He was a uniquely talented pastor and scholar.

We have briefly covered some of the philosophical contributions Edwards made. Masterpieces like *Freedom of the Will*, ironically penned in a fortified enclosure in the New England wilderness, established Edwards in his day as America's foremost philosopher. Over 250 years later in an age that boasts a much livelier academic climate, no American has surpassed Edwards in this field.

We have looked extensively at Edwards's sermons.

Regardless of background or conviction, one cannot help but marvel at Edwards's preaching. As he honed his writing style, Edwards became a masterful preacher, able to simultaneously enlighten the mind, sear the heart, and stir the soul. The sermons that produce this effect, often spanning ten to twenty single-spaced pages of text, pack more punch than many full-length books. To put it succinctly, Edwards was one of the most able preachers of Christian history.

We have also observed Edwards's ability as a theologian. His work in texts like *Distinguishing Marks* sets him apart as a skillful, biblically oriented thinker. In a number of areas—salvation, holiness, and the afterlife, among others—Edwards distinguished himself as a rigorous and insightful theologian. He made his mark in this role, we might note, in the context of pastoral ministry.

As the story of Edwards's life has unfolded, we have also seen other roles Edwards filled in his busy life—husband, father, college president, mentor. We have seen that Jonathan Edwards was a uniquely gifted man who accomplished a great deal in the time given him by the Lord. The Northampton pastor was a choice servant of God.

In seeking the essence of Edwards, though, we have argued that he was, at his core, nothing more than a Christian man. This is not to minimize him. We have in fact taken pains to explore his multidimensionality and to benefit from it. But we have suggested that Edwards's identity centered in his Christian identity. Jonathan Edwards was fundamentally a Christian man. He lived for the glory of God. Throughout his life, he woke each morning with a thirst to magnify the Lord who had saved his soul from hell and given him eternal life. His days were filled with activity toward that end. If we do not understand anything else about Jonathan Edwards, we should understand that. He was a Christian—not a super-Christian, not a man who walked an inch off of the ground, but a believer in the Lord Jesus Christ who fought the same fight we do and loved the same God we love.

If we would home in on the essence of Edwards, we would do well to home in on the essence of his faith. The pastor lived a great life because he worshipped a great God and savored that reality each day that he lived. In his mind, God loomed large over the great and small things of life, directing them according to an all-wise providence. He was not limited or weak. He was magnificent, and He gave his creation the opportunity to taste the goodness of life lived for Him. He had spoken to humanity in His Word, enabling all who yearned after a savior to find Him in the revelation that disclosed the person and work of Jesus Christ. At its core, Edwards's existence centered around a personal God who offered atoning salvation to a fallen race through His inspired Word. So too must ours, for our justification and our delight.

The life and thought of Jonathan Edwards calls us to emulate him today. Living in a very different world, with unique challenges and opportunities, we have the same ability to seize life for the glory of God. We who love and worship Jesus Christ will find Him just as satisfying in our modern era as Edwards did in his own day. May we learn from his example, glean his wisdom, and above all, devote ourselves to pursuing our great God on a daily basis just as Jonathan Edwards, lover of God, did so many years ago.

Acknowledgments

*W*e have a number of people to thank for the production of this volume.

We would like to thank Dave DeWit of Moody Publishers. Dave is an excellent editor and has been a tremendous help and encouragement in all aspects of the process. It was Dave who suggested that this project encompass not one book, but five, forming a comprehensive and definitive introductory series. We are thankful for his vision. We would also thank Chris Reese, who gave excellent feedback on this and every manuscript and made each book clearer and better.

We would like to thank Dr. John Piper for graciously providing a series foreword. It is a signal honor to have Dr. Piper involved in this project. Dr. Piper has enriched our understanding of Jonathan Edwards as he has for countless people. We are thankful to the Lord for his ministry, and we deeply appreciate his commendation of this collection. We are thankful as well for the assistance of David Mathis, Executive Pastoral Assistant to Dr. Piper.

We owe a debt of gratitude to our wives, Bethany Strachan and Wilma Sweeney, who bore the weight of this project with us. We would like to thank good friends who gave encouragement and counsel at various points in the project. Jed Coppenger, David Dykes, Adam Embry, Greg Gilbert, Brad Wheeler, Matt Hall, Ben Dockery—thank you.

We thank no one more in an earthly sense than Andy and Donna Strachan and David Sweeney. Dad and Mom, your son thanks God for you every day that he lives. Your love for the Lord enabled him to taste the love of the Lord, just as Jonathan's parents introduced him to vibrant Christianity. David Sweeney, you are a great son. Your father loves you dearly, and looks forward to seeing how the Lord will use you for His purposes in days to come.

Above all others, we thank our great God, through whom this book is written, to whom it is devoted, for whom it is offered.

Recommended Resources on Jonathan Edwards

*F*or the premier collection of Edwards's own writings, see *The Works of Jonathan Edwards*, vol. 1–26, Yale University Press. Access these works in their entirety free of charge at http://edwards.yale.edu.

For secondary sources, we recommend the following.

Introductory Reading

Byrd, James P. *Jonathan Edwards for Armchair Theologians.* Louisville, KY: Westminster John Knox Press, 2008.

McDermott, Gerald R. *Seeing God: Jonathan Edwards and Spiritual Discernment.* Vancouver: Regent College Publishing, 2000.

Nichols, Stephen A. *Jonathan Edwards: A Guided Tour of His Life and Thought.* Phillipsburg, NJ: Presbyterian & Reformed, 2001.

Storms, Sam. *Signs of the Spirit: An Interpretation of Jonathan Edwards' Religious Affections.* Wheaton, IL: Crossway Books, 2007.

Deeper Reading

Gura, Philip F. *Jonathan Edwards: America's Evangelical.* New York: Hill & Wang, 2005.

Kimnach, Wilson H., Kenneth P. Minkema, and Douglas A. Sweeney, eds. *The Sermons of Jonathan Edwards: A Reader.* New Haven: Yale University Press, 1999.

Lesser, M. X. *Reading Jonathan Edwards: An Annotated Bibliography in Three Parts, 1729–2005.* Grand Rapids: Eerdmans, 2008

Marsden, George. *Jonathan Edwards: A Life.* New Haven: Yale University Press, 2003.

McDermott, Gerald R., ed. *Understanding Jonathan Edwards: An Introduction to America's Theologian.* New York: Oxford University Press, 2009.

Moody, Josh. *The God-Centered Life: Insights from Jonathan Edwards for Today.* Vancouver: Regent College Publishing, 2007.

Murray, Iain H. *Jonathan Edwards: A New Biography.* Edinburgh: Banner of Truth Trust, 1987.

Piper, John. *God's Passion for His Glory: Living the Vision of Jonathan Edwards.* Wheaton, IL: Crossway Books, 1998.

————, and Justin Taylor, eds. *A God Entranced Vision of All Things: The Legacy of Jonathan Edwards.* Wheaton, IL: Crossway Books, 2004.

Smith, John E., Harry S. Stout, and Kenneth P. Minkema, eds. *A Jonathan Edwards Reader.* New Haven: Yale University Press, 1995.

Sweeney, Douglas A. *Jonathan Edwards and the Ministry of the Word: A Model of Faith and Thought.* Downers Grove, IL: InterVarsity Press, 2009.

BRINGING YOU THE TIMELESS CLASSICS
Classics

... these are key books that every believer on the journey of spiritual formation should read.

Holiness
ISBN-13: 978-0-8024-5455-3

Born Crucified
ISBN-13: 978-0-8024-5456-0

Names of God
ISBN-13: 978-0-8024-5856-8

The Overcoming Life
ISBN-13: 978-0-8024-5451-5

All of Grace
ISBN-13: 978-0-8024-5452-2

The Secret
of Guidance
ISBN-13: 978-0-8024-5454-6

The Incomparable Christ
ISBN-13: 978-0-8024-5660-1

Orthodoxy
ISBN-13: 978-0-8024-5657-1

The Apostolic Fathers
ISBN-13: 978-0-8024-5659-5

MOODY
PUBLISHERS
MoodyClassics.com